Not All Violins

Spiritual Resources by Women with Disabilities and Chronic Illnesses

The Barb Wire Collective

Charlotte Caron

Gail Christy

Sharon Davis

Mary Elford

Joan Heffelfinger

Elinor Johns

Christine Neal

Elizabeth Richards

Jayne Whyte

United Church Publishing House
Toronto, Canada

Not All Violins
Spiritual Resources by Women with Disabilities and Chronic Illnesses

Copyright © 1997 The United Church Publishing House

All biblical quotations, unless otherwise noted, are from the *New Revised Standard Version Bible*, copyright © 1989, by the Division of Christian Education of the National Council of the Churches of Christ in the United States of America. Used by permission.

Care has been taken to trace ownership of copyright material contained in this text. The publisher will gratefully accept any information that will enable it to rectify any reference or credit in subsequent printings.

Canadian Cataloguing in Publication

Not all violins : spiritual resources by women with disabilities and chronic illnesses

Includes bibliographical references.
ISBN 1-55134-077-1
1. Physically handicapped - women Religious life. 2. Women and religion. 3. Discrimination against the handicapped. I. Caron, Charlotte. II. Barb Wire Collective
BV639.W7N68 1997   291.1'78324'082   C97-931247-7

United Church Publishing House
3250 Bloor Street West, Fourth Floor
Etobicoke, Ontario
Canada M8X 2Y4
416-231-5931
bookpub@uccan.org

Design and production: Department of Publishing and Graphics
Editor: Ruth Chernia

Printed in Canada
5 4 3 2 1   03 02 01 00 99 98

970134

This book is dedicated to the memory of

Barbara Elliott

and was made possible by a grant from her estate and with the support of her sisters Marg Manktelow and Betty White and many friends.

Contents

Introduction

How the Book Came to Be

This book was written out of the experience of nine Canadian women. All of us live with disabilities and/or chronic illnesses. All of us are women of faith. Some of us connect closely with or are employed by Christian churches; others of us see ourselves as people of faith without attachment to a traditional religious body. We offer our spiritual resources, assuming that experiences in our faith communities are shared by people with disabilities and chronic illnesses in many denominations, religious affiliations, or spiritual practices.

We have known richness and life and vision through our faith experiences. Yet we have not always been accepted and nurtured by our religious traditions. As women with disabilities and chronic illnesses, the theologies and spiritualities around us do not always fit us. Sometimes it is a challenge to hold onto faith.

We have chosen to come together to write about our lives because we believe that others will be enriched by sharing the spiritual paths on which we travel and rest. We have come to believe that we know the power of love and of the holy in new ways because of our experiences with our bodies and minds. We also invite those who live with able bodies or with short-term bodily injury or illness to join with us in compassion and in the struggle for justice for people with disabilities and chronic illnesses.

The book was made possible through a grant from the estate of Barbara Joan Elliott. Barb was a friend to most of us who have worked together on this project. The project honours the spirit of Barb Elliott and the book is dedicated in her memory. She struggled with a spirituality and theology that could speak to her as a woman with a disability. Our book carries on this quest that she did not complete in her lifetime and, in keeping with the spirit of her life, seeks to be a small contribution to justice for women.

Feminism, justice for women, and feminist theology were Barb's passions. She loved to discuss feminist theology and to do feminist analysis on every subject under the sun. For the year or two before her death, she focused much of her energy on the relationship of feminism and disability, and had just begun to push the theological questions towards what feminist theological resources are available to people who live with disabilities.

Barb also believed that we only do theology in community. Thus a feminist perspective and the collaborative approach to writing the book seem essential.

We believe the experiences of women, especially the experiences of women living with disabilities and chronic illnesses, need to be named and validated. Feminism is the process of seeking healing from personal pain and social injustice, and working for transformation towards community, equality, and inclusion. Feminism asserts the free and public participation of all people in decisions that will affect their lives. It affirms the goodness of creation and ourselves as women seeking a new politic and theology of gender relations. Or, as Mary Hunt states: "To be a feminist is to be committed to a lifelong struggle to bring about the sharing of power and the equitable distribution of resources."[1] We believe that feminism gives insight into the experience of living as women with disabilities and chronic illnesses in our society. We hope using these tools for change will allow the lives of women with disabilities and chronic illnesses to be improved.

A recurring theme in our conversations was that pity is not helpful. We believe that women with disabilities are important to the well-being of the world. The world needs us; it needs to listen to and learn from us. We are charting new territory, exploring new visions, and creating new spiritual resources.

Process

Nine women agreed to form the collective. Each of us wrote an article, or contributed resources or poetry about our lives. Some of us also wrote about our visions of what society could be like if our lives were taken seriously. The material we wrote individually was then distributed among us for reading. Subsequently we came together for a three-day consultation. All nine women joined together at the beginning of the event although some had to leave for a variety of reasons before it ended. Those of us who live with the unpredictability of chronic illness felt it quite significant that all nine women were all able to complete the writing in a restricted time-frame and attend the consultation. At the consultation, we shared our responses to the articles, engaged in dialogue, laughed, and cried. After we returned to our homes, we rewrote and edited. Charlotte Caron agreed to pull the material together, and to write the additional chapters on the social construction of disability and the effect of Christian faith on our lives as women with disabilities and chronic illnesses, our learnings, and spiritual insights. Some months later, the draft manuscript was distributed to collective members for comment and editing.

A range of women participated. Several of us are in middle age; the youngest is 21. Our disabilities vary: two live with cerebral palsy, one with chronic fatigue syndrome, one with multiple disabilities, two with diabetes, one with severe hearing impairment, one with multiple personality (dis)order, one with Candida complex problems, and one with multiple sclerosis. Some reside in urban areas, some in rural areas; some call Saskatchewan home, some dwell elsewhere. Some are employed in the paid work force; some are students; for some, health care is a full-time job. Some live in primary, partnered relationships; several have children—ranging in ages from young to adult; some are single by choice or circumstance. Some of us knew each other before the consultation; some of us did not.

For some of us writing flows easily, but several mentioned that it happens painstakingly. Some find talking easier than writing. Writing can be difficult because of the level of vulnerability involved in speaking the truth and letting people know what life is really like. For some it is hard because of the nature of the disability with which we live, meaning concentration and the technical nature of writing take a lot of effort. For others filling a page with our thoughts and ideas is intimidating. All of us lived with some level of anxiety as we started into this project. Yet our lives are important. We needed to share the wisdom we have gained.

For many of us, the consultation provided a first opportunity to talk together in a group of women where we all identified ourselves as women with chronic illnesses and disabilities. We worked hard and we laughed a lot. We shared distressing stories about hurtful things that had happened around our disabilities and illnesses. When we shared the episodes with drama or named the things we wished we had said, or heard potential responses, we roared in healing laughter. Our lives and our disabilities/illnesses differ, but we shared faith, fury, and frustration in significant ways. This phrase of Elinor Johns is one that fit for many of the collective members. We felt safe together, trusting that we would not have to defend the vulnerable parts of our lives. One woman said, "I haven't had such a safe learning space for more than 20 minutes ever before!" It offered a good time to learn about self and others. The weekend was not easy—or, in the words of one participant, "I have yet to decide if it was wonderful!"

After the time together one woman wrote, "I felt so changed after the weekend with you. I felt I was understood and that my experiences were validated and shared by others. Because I felt so accepted by you, it is hard to continue to live in a world that has not changed. People still treat me the same."

Our power for change is important. We empowered each other. We confirmed that our strategies for coping with life in a disabling society offer rich and powerful resources worth sharing with others. Again and again we repeated Elinor's words, "Living with disability takes a lot of ability."

We decided to call ourselves "The Barb Wire Collective"—a good prairie image. Barb Elliot used the idea of an electric current as a connector that holds women together and empowers us. We thought of that kind of wire connector. And the barbs—the sharp jabs and points—seemed appropriate too. As well, we talked about boundaries and ways in which we can make safe spaces for women with disabilities and chronic illness. Jayne wrote more after the event:

> After the Spiritual Resources get-together weekend, I thought more about the name "Barb Wire Collective." In 1964, I was on a summer youth project in the ranching country near the Cypress Hills. The households actually used their barbed wire fences as telephone lines. At gates, the top strand was often guided up and down tall posts to ensure that connections would not be broken. When the phones were not working, they would go out and check their fence lines.
>
> One household had two phones, the local barbed wire line and the Saskatchewan Telephone connection. The provincial telephone company insisted that their phone be installed far enough away that there could be no hook-up between the two systems. So the woman in the house with two phones would take messages in her kitchen and run to the phone in the living room to pass them on.

I noticed similarities between this image and the discussions that we shared over the weekend. In a way, developing this book is like creating our own network using what we have and what we have learned. The recurring theme of boundaries in our discussion correlates with maintaining lines of communication, as well as the breakdown in contacts when a fence line was broken or a gate left open. Many of our frustrations result because the distance is too great between our needs and the general system. And all of the women in the collective (including Barb) have spent much of our lives running back and forth, carrying messages, sharing stories, and providing education and support to people who share our lives (lines) and those who control the access (the provincial telephone system).

We had talked about obvious metaphors in the name "Barb Wire Collective." We had acknowledged the influence of Barb Elliott. We had thought of fences that keep things in, keep things out. We had noticed the need for barbs to increase the protection and scratch the intruders. We had talked about being "wired" with energy, anger, fatigue, and coffee. This is our Barb Wire connection.

Barb's questions were always before us as we worked on the project.

- What are the alternatives?
- Who would benefit from this?
- What will this mean for women?
- Which women?
- Where would power be?
- What would it mean if we could be in solidarity with women around the globe working to transform radically the structures in which we live our lives?
- How do we maintain self respect?
- Do I have intrinsic value as being in God's image?
- How do I want to spend these last days?
- Can I live with integrity as if I have an open-ended future?
- Do we as women living with disabilities and chronic illnesses benefit society?
- Should it not be possible for everyone to have what they need to be out and about?

- We are constantly caught up in doing the accommodating to other people; when is it the community's responsibility to accommodate?
- How can we live maximally in an ongoing way especially as disability increases?

Structure of the book

After the Introduction, two chapters follow on how society constructs our views of disabilities and chronic illnesses and on the role of Christianity in creating views and attitudes about disability and chronic illness. Stories and materials written by each of the women in the Collective appear next. As well, a chapter was compiled from pieces that Barb Elliott wrote during her lifetime. A chapter composed of a conversation that occurred at the consultation follows. The next chapter summarizes some of our learnings, strategies, and resources. Because vision creates important links in our spirituality, some visions are intertwined with the chapters written by the women and some appear in a chapter immediately prior to the conclusion.

The forms of writing in the chapters differ. This seems significant. Women with disabilities and chronic illnesses have different abilities. Reading prose text is a problem for some, so poetry, reflections, and dialogue are included. For some theory helps understanding; for others shared experience enriches more. Some will want or need sections read aloud, and therefore we have used subheadings to divide longer pieces into manageable parts. While for some readers the mixed media of the book may be distracting, we think it symbolic of the real differences among women living with disabilities and chronic illnesses. For readers with able bodies and minds, we invite you to recognize that what for some may be preference, for others is necessity.

Disabling Ideas
The Social Construction of Disability

What We Believe about How Society Works

How a society thinks about, names, and portrays disability creates an environment that affects the lives of people with disabilities in that society. What a society values of architecture, living configurations, employment, and recreation can enhance or detract from the lives of people with disabilities and chronic illnesses.

Little of the social and physical construction of North American society gives encouragement to people who live with disabilities. Mark Rosentraub and John Gilderbloom ask, "Why do we not build our facilities to meet the needs of people with some limitations? The usual response is that it costs too much. It is our contention, however, that we are socialized not to think about people with limitations."[2] Many of the things that people with disabilities need and want are simple things. Yet we are not always considered in social planning. Systemic barriers and lack of recognition create discrimination and, often, poverty.

As well, the media provide few positive images of people with physical or mental disabilities. Few major characters in ordinary

television shows, talk-show hosts, or newscasters are persons
with visible disabilities. When a movie portrays someone with a
disability or when an organization uses an advertising campaign to
raise research or support funds, people with disabilities are usually
portrayed either as heroes or as objects needing charity. Few
media images show ordinary people with disabilities doing
ordinary things with non-disabled people. Even fewer images of
people whose disabilities require them to have assistance to
function and survive, or whose bodies are shaped contrary to the
media norm, appear. We receive few images and models of how
to live fulfilling and good lives if we have disabilities or chronic
illnesses.

Disability is a social construct. The society in which we live
creates the way we view people with disabilities. Our
understandings are not biologically "given." The current dominant
social view of disability in North America is that people with
disabilities and chronic illnesses should be invisible and powerless.

Anthropologist Mary Douglas addresses the fact that society
determines how the physical body will be perceived in any culture.
Her research indicates that the way bodies move, sit, and rest; the
forms of care we give to our body through grooming, feeding, and
exercise; and the pain bodies can tolerate are cultural categories.
The individual body in any culture learns to conform to the
cultural norms established by that culture.

She goes on to note that where there is little concern for social
boundaries, there is little concern for bodily boundaries.
Hierarchies are created through the culturally determined
relationships of head to feet, of brain and sexual organs, of mouth
and anus. Bodies are to be controlled in ways that allow for the
hierarchies to be maintained. Both social forms and ideology are
constructed to reinforce the hierarchies of bodily control.
Douglas goes on, "Bodily control will be appropriate where
formality is valued, and most appropriate where the valuing of
culture above nature is most emphasised."[3]

Although she does not speak specifically about the situation of
people with disabilities, what she says is significant. Our society

expects people to control their bodies: control their weight, control when and where they eliminate waste from their bodies, control bodily odour and functions. Expectations are set about what clothing people wear for given occasions, and how bodies move in relation to people with physical, economic, social, or sexual power. Most people with physical disabilities and chronic illnesses cannot control their bodies: their body image, when their bodies will work well and when they will not, or what they might do. Most people with mental illnesses cannot control their thoughts. Most people with other mental disabilities cannot adapt to the social controls that are expected in society. In a society that values control and power, lives that cannot be controlled are devalued or ignored or punished. North American political thought and theology focus on those who can keep their bodies and minds under control. Sue Wendell challenges this focus on control, suggesting that when societies idealize the body, people begin to believe they can control their bodies. People who cannot control their bodies are seen as failures and often feel like failures. She adds: "When you listen to this culture in a disabled body, you hear how often health and physical vigour are talked about as if they were moral virtues. People constantly praise others for their 'energy,' their stamina, their ability to work long hours."[4]

We believe that the way society thinks about bodily control and about people with disabilities and chronic illnesses must change. Social and media images, political thought, and theology all need to move from a construct of control to a system of acceptance and diversity where all people affected participate in the naming and the shaping of the common good. Society can be reconstructed in ways that value people with various physical and mental disabilities and illnesses, and place us within the circle rather than at the bottom of a hierarchical heap.

Our Relationships with Our Bodies

Living with a disabled body proves a challenging feat in a society constructed for young, able-bodied people who have power and strength. Feminist theory and theology often celebrate the body.

Embodiment constitutes a critical theme in feminism, countering the dualistic and patriarchal notion that the mind is more important than the body. For example, feminist theologian, Mary Hunt rightly claims that women's friendships are implicitly physical. "Whether we touch, mime, eat, cuddle, exercise, talk, play, make love, comfort, imbibe, relax, watch movies, massage, pray, sleep, or celebrate, virtually every relational act is a physical event, something mediated by our bodies." To name this embodiment is essential because traditional theological writing has ignored the physical nature of humanity.[5]

Our bodies are ourselves. But this may be a more comfortable thought for able-bodied women than for women with disabilities. Browne, Connors, and Stern indicate the ambivalence that our embodiment causes for us noting that our bodies are precious, and yet they are the focus of pain, causing us to live as if our bodies were separate from ourselves. We have to value ourselves enough to take care of ourselves. Yet "[s]ometimes we feel as though our bodies are trying to kill us. They betray us in our struggle to resist patriarchal desires for 'feminine weakness.'"[6]

When our patriarchal society devalues our bodies, it remains hard for us to respect them and regard them highly. Yet when the feminist movement says that our bodies are of utmost importance, we again feel that bodies with disabilities are not the ones being valued. Our ambivalence about our bodies is real.

Language

We noted above that the way we name and describe people and situations affects their lives. We choose to use the term people with disabilities or a person living with [the name of the particular disability or chronic illness]. Placing the person before the disability is intentional. First we are first people with a variety of skills, gifts, and life experiences. Our disabilities and chronic illnesses do not comprise who we are. They create part of our reality, but only part. When we use mechanical and technical aids to assist our living, we try to be clear that the person remains central, and that the technical aid is used by the person to assist her or his life. For example, we would say a person using a wheelchair or a woman who communicates by using a computer.

Much discussion occurs in the community of people with disabilities and chronic illnesses about what names are appropriate. It is our contention that no one definition fits. We want the power to be self-defining and self-identified, to do our own naming rather than to be defined and named by those who have power in society.

Some people accept the World Health Organization definitions as a useful starting place:

> *Impairment* is defined as a loss or abnormality of psycho-logical, physiological, or anatomical structure or function which may be permanent or transitory. ...
>
> A *disability* is any restriction or lack, resulting from the impairment, of an ability to perform an activity in the manner or within the range considered normal. ...
>
> *Handicaps* limit or prevent a person from fulfilling a role that is normal depending on age, sex, or cultural factors.[7]

Some things offend us. "Gimp," "cripple," "victim," "afflicted with" are not acceptable. We want these wiped from human vocabulary! Most of us dislike "handicapped" because of its origins in the time when people with disabilities and illnesses had no way to make a living other than to be street vendors—selling pencils or begging and asking people to put coins in their "handy" caps that they held out to passers-by. However, some current writers use handicap as a description of the oppression caused to people with disabilities by the able-bodied population.[8] Jane Field elaborates:

> I am not handicapped. Society is handicapped when it shuts out people like me. I am not physically challenged. Tri-athletes and mountain climbers are physically chal-lenged. And I'm certainly no more differently-able than anyone is from anyone else. No. I simply have a disabil-ity.[9]

Medical Perceptions

Medical practices frequently reinforce the current social views of people with chronic illnesses. When illness strikes, people generally assume that it will be short-term and that recovery will happen, that it is an interruption in one's life. Most of the medical profession and many individuals see illness as something to struggle against and defeat.

Our social norms about bodily control invite us to act as if illness were acute and not chronic. Even when people acquire what is known to be a chronic illness, they may expect their physician to cure them. They may expect to retrieve their past healthy self. Often a person with a chronic illness uses medical compliance and feels betrayed when "compliance does not pay off in recovery."[10] Becoming a good patient is a tactic for many people with chronic illnesses who live with a medical model that indicates that if you do the right things and obey doctor's orders, you will get well; you will regain control of your body/life. Unfortunately, as Susan Wendell notes, a heroic approach to medicine does not help people consider "how to live with long-term or life-threatening illness, how to communicate with doctors and nurses and medical bureaucrats about these matters, how to live with limitations, uncertainty, pain, nausea, and other symptoms when doctors cannot make them go away."[11]

No reason exists to assume that chronic illnesses and disabilities are medical conditions or that they should necessarily be stigmatizing. Social construction creates the oppression and discrimination.

Discrimination and Access Issues

All disabled people experience discrimination. Many people feel a list of politically correct disabilities exists. Some disabilities are seen as more noble (or less disfiguring) than others, and some get considerably more attention in funding and research programs.

We recognize the problem of hierarchies in the midst of our oppression. We believe that the perpetuation of hierarchies creates horizontal violence, which is what happens when groups with little power are set up to fight against each other. Horizontal violence usually happens when the dominant model is based in competition and limiting resources. For example, in Canada, governments limit research funding. This means that those involved in AIDS research are in competition for funds with those involved in research for breast cancer cures. These two groups have been known to fight with each other about whose research is more important while the government continues to cut funding. Native, Inuit, and Métis groups are also encouraged to fight among themselves while the government continues to serve the interests of the dominant society and limit with which First Nations groups it will negotiate. If the powerless groups are distracted into fighting and competing with each other for the crumbs, they do not have time and energy to put into addressing the injustices caused and perpetuated by those who hold power.

For justice to occur, those who have little power now need access and power to participate in the decisions that affect their lives. However most of the ideology of North America is based in competition and hierarchy, and thus it is perceived that if horizonal violence were limited, vertical violence would increase (i.e., the powerless would become violent against the powerful). There is no thought that the reason for horizontal violence is lack of needed resources and that in a just society where everyone had what they needed for sustainable life, power could be shared among many.

All of us who have disabilities and chronic illness live in this world together. If those who control economic, political, and social power can keep us fighting with each other about who is worse off, they free themselves from doing anything that takes our needs seriously . They can ignore the fact that as women and as people with disabilities and chronic illnesses, we are disempowered in North American society.

Empowerment changes our ideas about powerlessness. We recognize that systemic forces oppress us rather than our personal problems. Then we act to change the conditions of our lives. Empowerment for us would change the nature and

distribution of power in particular cultural contexts so that
women with disabilities and chronic illnesses would become
creators of culture. We need to work together for access to the
resources all humans need for full and enriching lives. We also
need advocates among the powerful.

The feminist movement has not always taken seriously the
differences within it. As a result, many women with disabilities
have chosen to be part of the disability rights movement rather
than the feminist movement. Adrienne Asch and Michelle Fine
point out that feminism challenges the social expectations placed
on women around marriage, child raising, and housekeeping. But,
they argue, many women with disabilities "have been warned by
parents that men only 'take advantage'; they have been sterilized
by force or 'choice,' rejected by disabled and non-disabled
heterosexual and lesbian partners, abandoned by spouses after
onset of disability, and thwarted when they seek to mother."[12]

Disabled girls and women do not necessarily see what they
have in common with those able-bodied women who have
dominated the feminist community. But, in fact, women with
disabilities and chronic illnesses do less well than men with
disabilities in terms of education, employment, medical and
research programs, and community services. Violence against
women and lack of sexual information and choices also link
women with disabilities and chronic illnesses to all women.

Browne, Connors, and Stern outline some of the bottom-line
needs for women with disabilities and chronic illnesses, including
removal of communication, transportation, and architectural
barriers. They note that society's barriers rather than our
conditions disable. "To consider it a special privilege to use a
telephone, ride a bus or use a public bathroom is absurd." They
state that such things as curb-cuts and telephone amplification
devices should be routinely available, but note that accessibility
involves attitudes as well as functions. Freedom to make "the
same choices accorded to able-bodied people" forms part of the
requirement for access.[13]

These agendas need to be linked to other agendas within the

feminist movement, and women with disabilities and chronic illnesses as well as our advocates need to make our voices heard in determining priorities and strategies for social change.

Women in a Disabling Society

Disability is a phenomenon socially constructed to create hierarchies, to keep a powerful few in control of the resources that are needed by others for basic survival and for full and free life. The social construction of a world where a few powerful people and large systemic structures set the agendas, control the definitions of health, beauty, and goodness means that most people seek homogeneity: they seek to be as much like those in power as possible. Women with disabilities cannot succeed in such a system.

The norm has to be diversity and acceptance of difference for us to belong. We need freedom from hierarchical control, and freedom from the socially constructed demand to control our bodies to fit a norm we cannot achieve. As we participate in collective movements for justice, we recognize the ways in which we are encouraged towards horizontal violence rather than cooperation and interdependence. Because our society has disabled us, we are committed to visions of transformation. We long for a world where disabilities and chronic illnesses are seen as part of normal life and appropriate aids to living will be available to all. What is socially constructed can and will change.

Christianity
Disabling and Enabling Theologies

Christian faith comprises part of our experience. We speak of it for three reasons. First, all of us have some connections with the Christian church in our past or present. Second, many people with disabilities have experienced the church as destructive to them and we want to acknowledge the churches' participation in that evil. Third, because Christianity dominates religious expression in Canada and has set the tone for much of the cultural life of North American society, we feel that even people who do not participate in Christian faith are influenced by it in our cultural milieu. We speak from what we know best but our perception says that Christianity is not worse or better than any other religion nor New Age philosophy of life.

Christianity has taken many forms in North America. It has espoused many values and ideologies about all of human life including illness and disability. Sometimes Christianity has devalued and ignored people with chronic illnesses and disabilities. Sometimes it has treated us as evil or sinful. Other times the church has been a place of inclusion, hope, and liberation. As Nancy Eiesland says,

No single story about the relationship between persons with disabilities and the Christian church can express our diverse, complex and enigmatic connection. This complicated bond underscores the ambiguities of our common life and highlights the tensions in beliefs about trust and suspicion, shame and affirmation, holiness and defilement, sin and grace.[14]

This chapter looks at several theological understandings that have been part of Christian theology in order to elaborate on the complicated bonds and ambiguities to which Eiesland refers.

One common theme emerges: disability and chronic illness are "God's will." This idea takes two forms—one, of punishment, the other of glorification. The former means that the individual (or their parents) sinned and thereby brought this "misfortune" on themselves through their disobedience to God. God is understood as an all powerful ruler; people are seen as inherently prone to evil and to disobedience. Even though God wills people to be good, they cannot do this and therefore must be punished for their sins. According to this theology, one form of punishment is physical, such as an incurable illness or disability in themselves or their children.

While at a logical level, many people would not accept such a theology, when they face the reality of late onset disability or chronic illness, or experience the birth of a child who has a disability, their question becomes, "What did I do to deserve this?" Many people blame themselves and search their lives for what they have done wrong to cause this to happen. They see it as punishment. The church has reinforced this point of view in many cases, especially when it has claimed, "If you have enough faith you will be well."

The flip side of the theme of disability as punishment grows out a theology of disability as God's will. Here God causes suffering in order to receive glory and praise. Some of us have had people say, "God must have had some purpose in mind by causing your illness." or "You are so noble to bear this cross." One of us was once invited to a Christian friend's home for coffee, only to discover when she arrived that a prayer group had assembled to drive the demons out of her life so she would be healed to the glory of God. In this theology, God again controls life, causing all things. However, in this case, God works in all things for good. If the person is open enough to following God's ways, she or he may be an inspiration to lead others to God, or may provide the opportunity for a miracle of God's healing power to be known.

We do not find these theological perspectives useful. In one, God is malicious. We cannot accept an avenging God. In the other view, God is selfish. We cannot believe that God manipulates people for God's self-glorification.

Another of the strains of theology that has been harmful to people with disabilities, especially women with disabilities, grows out of dualism. Put simply, this dualistic theology says that everything divides into either/or categories such as good and evil, God and humanity, spirit and body, heaven and earth/nature, perfect and imperfect, male and female. Unfortunately, women with disabilities always end up on the "evil" side of the equation: imperfect human female bodies on this earth. Christine Smith notes how readily women accept dualist thinking: "When we hate our bodies, it is easy to feel that they are the enemy and that the way to escape them is to transcend them spiritually."[15]

Like a theology that stresses disability and chronic illness as God's will, a theology that encourages us to ignore our bodily experiences and to hate our bodies is not constructive. We women with disabilities and chronic illnesses cannot afford to disconnect from our bodies; our bodies need our constant attention and care if we are to survive. We also have trouble with the concept of a God separate from our lives "above" the earthly matters of our daily lives. We are appalled by the idea of a God who might see us as evil simply because we are women with disabilities and chronic illnesses unable to live apart from the concrete existence we have here and now.

A third kind of theology stresses the goodness of patient, silent suffering. This theology claims that we all have troubles in this world and that those who bear their sufferings patiently will be rewarded in heaven. Patient suffering usually means that the people who suffer are not supposed to complain nor to express what is needed to make life easier. They are encouraged to identify with Jesus' suffering on the road to Calvary and on the cross. Some people who hold this theology believe that the more you suffer, the better a Christian you are. Faith is seen as living in brokenness and bearing your suffering quietly and alone.

Obviously this theology has been used by the powerful to control the less powerful in many ways: to perpetuate slavery, to deprive the poor of their right to decent standards of living, and to keep people with disabilities and chronic illnesses from having access to the resources we need for full life in society. Although theologically it articulates a premise of reward for virtuous suffering, politically it silences the voices of the powerless and maintains the positions of the powerful. Its paternalistic image of God as one who will give rewards to the deserving at the end of the race of life satisfies few.

A fourth example of Christian theology that has been used focuses on mission. In this understanding, churches help the needy and less fortunate of the world. Without doubt, many people with disabilities and chronic illnesses have been grateful for the charity, assistance, and outreach provided by churches. Nonetheless, this view has perpetuated the division between those who are the givers of charity and those who are the receivers. Often the recipients have become the objects of charity, not seen as persons with rights, personalities, and preferences. We become problems to be fixed, focuses for doing acts of kindness, silent and grateful participants in God's mission. Charity takes many forms including money, help with tasks, and advice. When Jean Blomquist became chronically ill in midlife, she found it very discouraging. She says she prayed; she cried; she went to doctors who told her to take vacations. She goes on:

> Friends and acquaintances offered advice: "Quit your job," "Take this vitamin," "Change your attitude," "Try this diet." Some, reflecting the shadow side of the wholistic

health orientation, asked, "What haven't you worked through?" implying that illness always reflects psychological or emotional disturbance, while health reflects physical, spiritual, and emotional balance and harmony. Those asking this question, of course, were physically healthy. Job's friends, I quickly learned, are still alive and well today.[16]

Joan, in our collective, describes the same phenomenon:

An example of grace is how Jesus was with people who had chronic illness or disability. He did not assume he knew what they needed. I think of the story of Jesus with the man who was blind and was begging. Jesus asked him, "What do you need?" I have so much respect for people who ask me what I need, and so much frustration with people who assume they know what I need without checking it out.

Being the object of charity, of others' assumptions that they know what is best for you, is no more helpful than being blamed for your situation. However, the image of God improves somewhat, to that of a benevolent giver, a kind God rather than a punitive or disinterested or rewarding God.

Nancy Eiesland helpfully claims,

As long as disability is addressed in terms of the themes of sin-disability conflation, virtuous suffering, or charitable action, it will be seen primarily as a fate to be avoided, a tragedy to be explained, or a cause to be championed rather than an ordinary life to be lived.[17]

Again Joan reflects her understanding,

I see much of the way Jesus interacted with people who had chronic illnesses or disabilities as being grace-filled. He confronted the life-denying attitudes of his day. For example, John's gospel tells of a man who was blind, the crowds assumed the man's parents must have sinned because the man was born blind. Jesus told them clearly that sin had nothing to do with it (John 9:1–5) It was no one's fault. I think we would do well to remember that. Still today, people say things like, "God must have had some purpose in mind by causing your diabetes." That kind of stuff is so annoying! Some things just happen. There is no logical explanation for it. God did not cause them. They just happen.

Our lives are very ordinary lives. We happen to live with disabilities and chronic illnesses. We are not solely defined by that reality. We are not being punished by God for something we did. We do not suffer to bring God glory. We are not bodies separate from spirits. We have no intention to be silent about our needs or to wait until heaven to have those needs met! We expect to be treated as fully human rather than as objects of charity. We just happen to be women who live with disabilities and chronic illnesses. For us, living with disabilities and chronic illnesses is not seen as an imperfection; it is normal life.

To claim this truth means Christianity needs to be explored from different perspectives than those above to bring any good news to the lives of people with disabilities.

First, a positive Christian faith means acceptance of the fact that people with disabilities and chronic illnesses are fully human, ordinary people. We believe that all people, including those with disabilities, are made in God's image. Whatever God is like, we are a part of that. "Our bodies participate in the *imago Dei*, not in spite of our impairments and contingencies, but through them."[18] We cannot know the fullness of God without acceptance of the lives of people with disabilities and chronic illness. To live in the image of God means self respect, acceptance, and using our unique gifts creatively and courageously in this world.

Christine Smith notes a consequence of accepting this theological premise. She claims that if we accept people with disabilities, that the North American myths of independence and rugged individualism will be exposed for what they are. No one always has control in this life. We are not always able to be powerful nor self-giving. All of us some of the time, and some of us all the time, need to receive care and assistance from others in order to function freely in society. This challenges the Christian adage that it is more blessed to give than to receive, more righteous to do the loving act than to be the recipient of that loving act.[19] To be equal in relationships means that we need both to give and to receive. We need to be subject of our own lives while at the same time refusing the myth of independence. Interdependence means we need each other in different ways.

In our collective, Joan also asserts the need to re-image God. Protestants value work highly. God works by creating, redeeming, sustaining. In the image of that Protestant God, many of us think that we are only valuable if we are working—and working hard. Joan adds,

> I know that is not a healthy attitude. It can be particularly alienating for those of us who, for one reason or another, are not working at a full-time, paying job. I find that I get caught in this trap sometimes. I want to prove that just because I have diabetes does not mean I cannot work just as hard as everyone else. When I add that to the fact the I am working at a job that is not traditionally considered a "woman's job" and the need to prove myself, I become a candidate for burnout.

Our image of God includes God at rest, at play, in recreative activity, in inactivity.

To understand ourselves as in the image of God also relocates sin. Instead of seeing the individual person who lives with a disability or chronic illness as sinful, sin is named as injustice against people with disabilities. To disrespect another human who is part of God's image is to sin.

And so, this theological understanding sees God as creator, as in relationship with all of creation, as incorporating reality. To be in the image of God is to be ourselves, that is, to be in relationship, to be engaged in the ebb and flow of care giving and care receiving, to create new standards for what creative life in relationship and at rest means.

Second, a positive Christian understanding means exploration of a liberatory theology. A key principle of liberation theology asserts that God is on the side of those who are oppressed and those who do not have power in society. God's aim for all of creation, including humanity, is justice: right relationship and well-being for all, life in all its fullness where people no matter what their class, race, physical or mental ability, sexual orientation, gender, or ethnic origin are empowered to be subjects of their own lives. Liberation theology is a materialist theology rooted in the concrete conditions of human life. This means that all work for justice addresses the real, lived inequities in this world. We examine, analyze, and protest against institutional arrangements that perpetuate and deepen social and economic inequality. Kwok Pui-lan states the norm from her perspective. It is not whether something appears in the Bible or comes from Augustine, Aquinas, Tillich, or Barth. For her:

> All theologies must be judged as to how far they contribute to the liberation and humanization of the human community. A living theology tries to bear witness to the unceasing yearning of human beings for freedom and justice, and articulates the human compassion for peace and reconciliation.[20]

Women with disabilities and chronic illnesses deserve justice. Nonetheless, oppression against women and against those with disabilities exists. Physical access and attitudinal acceptance form basic prerequisites for justice and liberation of women with disabilities and chronic illnesses. As Nancy Eiesland says,

> Many religious bodies have continued to think of and act as if access for people with disabilities is a matter of benevolence and goodwill, rather than a prerequisite for equality and the foundation on which the church as a model of justice must rest.[21]

Third, a constructive Christian faith requires a stance of solidarity. Solidarity means living as community and recognizing that we all are in this life together. All need to be included if the community is to be whole.

For many Christians, community has been understood as homogeneity. People can belong to the community if they assert the right beliefs and meet other cultural or religious criteria. Others are allowed in if they become "like us." But women with disabilities and chronic illnesses cannot fit into a homogeneous community. We embody difference and non-conformity to the cultural ideals. For us, pluralistic solidarity embodies a more constructive image of community than does homogeneity.

No one stream of Christian tradition has remained uniform through space and time. No single way of being a Christian community exists. At this point in history, differences in power mean that solidarity is limited.[22] The church that takes seriously diverse theologies recognizes that people with disabilities and chronic illnesses and other marginalized and oppressed people must become central to Christian life and mission.

Spaces for truth-telling about our lives are essential for solidarity and for justice. People have been taught by churches that respect means not asking about disabilities. This habit of ignoring denies how hard our lives are and allows other people off the hook from engaging with us about how their attitudes and practices affect us. Neither we nor other people benefit from this denial of reality.

Advocacy offers a more helpful stance. The Amanecida Collective describes what advocacy means to them.

> Our Christian/postchristian faith becomes increasingly an advocacy posture for the self-determination of all people who have been objectified and damaged by the imperialistic, racist, sexist, heterosexist, classist, and anti-Semitic deeds done 'in the name of Christ.' The Jesus of whom we speak in these pages, the one most of us in Amanecida call 'Christ', is no imperial sovereign. He is one who

stands beside us, by the power of the Spirit, and helps move the struggle for justice and peace along.[23]

An advocate stands with the less powerful and supports their interests, enables their self determination and works for their material, social, and political well-being.

We recognize that many women have been so hurt by Christianity—by theologies of punishment, glorification, dualism, patient suffering, and charity—that there is no possibility of knowing Christian faith as life giving. Others may find hope and strength through seeing ourselves in the image of God, being interdependent, re-imagining God, participating in a liberatory theological perspective, and being together in solidarity with each other and with advocates for justice.

Part of Who I am

Mary Elford *Speaks*

Webster's *New Collegiate Dictionary* (1981) defines a disability as the inability to pursue an occupation because of physical or mental impairment. It could also be a disqualification, restriction, or disadvantage. Disabilities appear as physical, mental, and spiritual, yet the effects that each disability has on the person's life are similar. Life with a disability is limited in some way. It is lacking in fullness and ease.

The most noticeable dis-ablings are physical, yet not all physical disability is immediately obvious. I, for example, do not usually think of myself as being disabled. I enjoy freedom of movement, I am active, and I do not look disabled. The condition that colours my living, which limits me, is partial nerve deafness. Because of the damaged nerves in my ears, I cannot hear many sounds without my hearing aids. Some of these sounds include whispers, bird songs, and various soft beeps and clicks of machinery. It is hard for me to hear children's voices. When I am in a situation with background noise, such as a large gathering of people, or a busy store, I strain to hear conversation. With a high volume of noise, I sometimes just give up. With my hearing aids, I can hear much more, but I still miss a great deal. My deafness limits my contact with people and with the world. It also helps to form the image that other people have of me. It informs my own self-image.

Many theological issues come to mind. I list some here. What is the worth of a person? Are some people worth more than others? Does God love non-disabled people more? Are disabled people loved more because they must be stronger to cope with life? Is it more important to be nice, or nicer to be important? What part of a person is emphasized? Why do we deny some parts of ourselves and play up other parts? Are not all parts created and thus good? How much does it cost to be generally even-tempered? How much does it benefit? Why do we try to earn love from God and from humans? Do we also try to earn our love of ourselves? How important is community and the inclusion of those on the fringes and margins? How may we emphasize "I–Thou" relations with other persons, rather than "I–it" relations with our disability? What place does anger have in my life with a disability?

We learn very early to pretend that disabilities and differences do not exist. Where they must be acknowledged, we see only the disability and not the person. I have seen many people stare at someone using crutches or a wheelchair. My first hearing aid was a box attached to my shirt, with a wire going to my ear. The box was probably not as monstrous as I thought, but I would not wear it, and so it could not help me. I did not want to be 'different.'

When we focus on the difference, we make that the most important and interesting feature of the person. Sometimes, after someone notices my hearing aids, their only concern is with some facet of my life as a hearing-impaired person. This is a part of my life, but it is nowhere near all of my life. There are many interesting things about me, but a focus on my disability leaves them all in the background.

It is more helpful when others recognize the disability and include it as part of the person's life and growth. If my parents had chosen to proclaim that there was nothing wrong with me instead of accepting that I could not hear, I might have acquired more of a sense that there was definitely something wrong somewhere. I think that this lie is harmful. If, for instance, my parents had ignored my non-response to whispers, they would not have had my hearing assessed, or tried hearing aids, or looked at a residential school for the deaf, or told my teachers at the public schools I attended that I needed a little bit of help. With this attitude, I might have wondered why there was so much wrong with the rest of the world, since I was obviously perfect. This chip on my shoulder would not have been terribly helpful in everyday life.

A constant struggle for me, and I suspect for many other deaf and hard-of-hearing people, lies with my own sense of self-worth. I know that levels of hearing and intelligence are not connected, but I often feel stupid because I cannot hear. It hurts me when people laugh at my inappropriate remarks, or when they refuse to say things again for me. When I am excluded from a group, I have learned a variety of responses. Depending on my energy level and interest, I may continue to try to be part of the group; I may paste a smile on my face and stand just outside of the group; I may quietly wander away and do something else; or I may wander away in pain and anger and frustration. All of these options leave me aching, feeling small and unimportant. I choose not to create a scene and demand inclusion. To me, that route invites condescension and pity. However, I also choose to give as little of myself to such excluding groups as I possibly can.

I find that pity is not helpful. An attitude of "Oh, what an awful thing you have to put up with!" focuses on the disability and on the things that I cannot do. I prefer to acknowledge that I cannot do some things, and then get on with the things that I can do. Compassion, however, is very helpful. It involves accepting that I am not capable of certain things, and celebrating with me the things that I can do. For example, someone who looks at me with pity may comment on how wonderfully well I get along, considering how little I can hear. A compassionate person will repeat things I do not hear, and make an extra effort to include me. Pity has a negative focus, seeing the disability first, while compassion feels more positive by seeing the whole person.

Compassion does not, however, let me become ungrateful or expecting or self-pitying. It lifts me up, and helps me to become a better person.

Deafness, like any other disability, has the potential to cause a great deal of anger. The frustration that other people show as they tire of repeating things for me is equalled by my frustration with them. I wonder why I always have to ask, as though I have or am the problem. Why can they not say it clearly the first time, or go with me to a more quiet location, or write it down, or use different-sounding synonyms?

I think anger around disability takes place because the other person or people become insecure around my imperfection. They may resent the extra effort and attention it takes to include me. They may be afraid of something they know little about or they may fear that it is contagious. They may have given it no thought and simply do not care. This anger can take concrete form in exclusion or in action. Exclusion occurs when I am snubbed, ignored, or otherwise left out of the group. Action is a more direct and obvious angry response. It could involve taunts, nicknames, or being made the butt of a joke. The result of any show of anger is usually more anger in response, and so the cycle continues.

I sometimes become angry because I can not hear. This anger gets directed at myself, or at the measles that robbed me of my hearing, or at God for having allowed it all to happen. I sometimes get angry with the world, because I must expend so much energy and emotion as I struggle for what so many people accept with unconscious ease. It is not wrong for me to be angry. If I use my anger, and do some good or creative thing, such as writing a poem, or broadening my understanding of other people with disabilities, the anger is not wrong. If, however, I choose to spiral downward through anger and depression to slosh about in self-pity, then my use of anger is wrong. Anger can point me towards life or towards death.

If I direct my anger towards God, that is not wrong. I do not need to protect God from my anger. I know that God does not cause bad things. When bad things like accidents or disease happen, God is not testing us or acting in malice. I believe that God is love, and all that God does is in love. I believe that God cries with me in my pain, and that God works with me to bring good from my situation. Because I cannot hear well, I have learned to concentrate on what I can hear. I have learned to listen, and this gift helps me to build strong individual relationships. I do not expect God to move in and fix everything. God is the source of life. An important part of human life is our free will, which gives us the choice of following God or our own way. This means that we must live with the consequences of our actions. If I am more honest and specific, I admit that I am not angry with God, but rather angry because God, too, is powerless.

It takes a great deal of energy for me to cope with not hearing well. It costs a lot to concentrate on sounds, and to continue to interact with people who have hurt me before. It would be much easier to growl and be nasty, or to just simply withdraw. I do these things, sometimes, if I don't have the energy, the time, or the desire to work at understanding. However, if I always choose to act in these ways, I build walls between me and other people. It can get pretty lonely in here, all by myself. I choose, most of the time, to take the walls down and be with other people in their humanity and mine.

Sometimes I focus on what is wrong with me, rather than on all that is right. I am learning, slowly, that I have worth because I am a child/creation of God, as I am and as I may become. I do not have worth because I earn it, but rather because God created me. There is nothing 'wrong' with me. I have limits like everyone else. I am human.

I close with something that demanded that I get out of bed and put it on paper back in 1989.

What is deafness?

It is not hearing, not understanding the spoken word, not fully comprehending.

It is misunderstanding. It is jumping into a conversation with what you think is a contribution, only to realize from the confused looks that you have misunderstood yet again.

It is pain. It is frustration when someone refuses to repeat something for you. It is withdrawing into silence, pretending that it doesn't matter that conversation is flowing over you.

It is gratitude, when someone cares enough to include you, even when you are feeling most sorry for yourself, and don't want to be included.

It is being socially inept, unable to make small talk, because everything you can hear must be important. You can hear so little, that anything that reaches your brain by way of your ears must be treasured.

It is coping with people who mumble and keep their hands in front of their faces and talk the other way.

In church, it is missing what are probably beautiful prayers, because custom dictates that you must bow your head and shut your eyes.

It is thankfulness for the hearing you do have. In some ways it might be easier to be totally deaf, but you can't imagine that.

It is thankfulness for technology that can help.

It is thankfulness for people who care.

It is not trusting your ears. When crossing the street, it is checking both ways with your eyes, to confirm that no traffic is approaching.

It is not listening to the radio for the words of the songs, but for the beat of the music.

It is not understanding television or movies. It is kind people who don't mind repeating salient portions of dialogue.

Deafness is not stupidity. Just because you cannot hear, does not mean you are mentally defective.

It is being sensitive to the facial expressions of people who don't know you, and matching them, to imply that your interested noises are conversation. This is so much easier on both of us than continually asking them to repeat themselves.

It is embarrassment, when the person catches on and chews you out.

It is sometimes getting a headache from concentrating so hard on those precious sounds.

It is a part of me.

Soaring and Comforting Wings
Joan Heffelfinger *Speaks*

I am a person who lives with diabetes. (Barb Elliott helped me to see the importance of respectful language around issues of chronic illness and disability.) For me, that means each day I take two injections of insulin—one before breakfast and one before supper. It also means that I check my blood by pricking my fingers four times a day, three days a week. As well, I have to be very careful about what and when I eat. Further, regular exercise and rest are essential for me.

In short, living with diabetes is something that I have to think about every day of my life. For instance, if I forget to eat when it is my snack time, I feel light-headed and shaky, and my speech becomes slurred. If I do not eat immediately, I run the risk of passing out.

Generally speaking, the fact that I have to think about my diabetes every day of my life is one about which people would rather not hear. As a woman, I have been taught that my thought processes and my body are two separate entities. I am not supposed to think about my body, but rather, to control it. However, I cannot control my body. The consequence is that I do not fit into society.

A related message that leads me to feel that I do not fit in has to do with what I perceive as the societal norm around illness. I believe that the norm is this: if you are sick, you are supposed to either get better or die. This is exemplified by the greeting cards that I received around the time I was diagnosed with diabetes. Most of them said, "Get well soon." People like me, who live with chronic illness or disability, do not fit into either of those categories.

Because I do not fit in, I have learned that I am supposed to be quiet about my diabetes. As a woman, I am not supposed to draw attention to myself except in certain stereotyped ways. In our society, women are encouraged to draw attention to their physical appearance (of course, only as it fits society's ideals), but not to their other gifts. However sometimes, in order to survive, I have to draw attention to myself. For instance, if I am at a meeting and it goes overtime, I may need to leave that meeting in order to get some food.

This struggle around not wanting to draw attention to myself is a complex one. I remember one time when I was in a gathering of friends and it was past my snack time. We were involved in a group ritual. I did not want to miss any of it. Neither did I want to draw attention to myself. I remember thinking to myself, "This will end soon. Surely I can last a few more minutes." So I stayed and got shakier and shakier and shakier. It got to the point where my need for food was so strong that I could not concentrate on what was going on.

Eventually, I had to remove myself from the scene in an attempt to meet my needs, but by then I was beyond the point of being able to help myself. I was mumbling, could not stand up, and clearly was desperate. When I get like that I have a hard time getting the words out to say what I need. It is as if my mind is in a haze, as if I am disconnected from my body. Part of me just wants to go to sleep, but another part of me knows that somehow I have to be able to get food. Another part of me just wishes people would know what I need at this point and get it without having to be told!

Fortunately some dear friends did rush around and get me some food after I managed to mumble that I needed food. By this time, everyone in the room knew there was something wrong. They could tell by the way I looked and by the look of panic on my friends' faces! Living with a chronic illness or disability makes life so complicated!

Given that mere survival is sometimes so difficult when one lives with a chronic illness, it can be an enormous challenge to think about how one might really live in a society that largely denies that people like me exist and does not accept that we have something worthwhile to contribute. In order to talk about how I can really live, I want to be clear about who I am. I am a feminist and a person of faith. For me, those two aspects of my personhood are intimately connected.

My faith is practised within the context of the Christian church. At the same time, it often transcends the bounds of what has traditionally been considered "Christian."

Being a feminist affects almost everything I do and almost everything I do not do. For me, feminism brings a critical or analytical perspective. Being a feminist enables me to analyze why our society is the way it is. It leads me to ask questions. Why is "fitting in" considered so important in our society? Why should I not draw attention to myself? Who benefits from a medical system that wants those of us with disabilities to get better or die? Who ever said it was me that needed "fixing" instead of society? Why is independence such a cherished concept? What about interdependence?

Some of these questions might make people feel uncomfortable, but so be it. Frank Chicane, a South African theologian said it well: "Until you start asking the questions that seem to be heretical, you haven't started grappling with the real issues." He was speaking on video about South Africa in 1989.

Being a feminist also helps me analyze why I am the way I am. It helps me figure out why I have the attitudes that I do towards my own body. I have incorporated some societal attitudes into my being because I am a part of society. One of those is that as a woman I am supposed to take care of everyone else first. Then maybe, if there is any time left over, I can take care of myself. My feminist analysis, however, teaches me that it is okay, indeed even good, to take care of my body. Being a feminist means I give myself permission to take care of myself.

Being a feminist also helps me to see that there is nothing wrong with asking for what I need. In fact, it is a wonderful idea! For example, if my blood sugar drops to a dangerous low, it is advisable to ask someone to get me some food. Further, I now let people with whom I am going to spend a fair amount of time know what diabetes means for me and how they can respond in helpful ways.

Not only my feminism but also my faith supports this point of view. A story from the Bible helps me to see that God delights in us when we ask for what we need. That story tells about a woman from Cana (Matthew 14:21–28) This persistent woman keeps asking Jesus for what she needs (the healing of her daughter) until she gets it. One of the things that I really like about this story is the part in which Jesus acknowledges that it is the woman's faith and determination that are necessary for healing to take place. At no point does Jesus claim that it is all because of him that she is healed. If she can be so clear about her needs and can make sure they get met, so too can I.

Another Bible passage resonates with me. Jesus says, "Love your neighbour as yourself (Matthew 19:19)." He does not say, "Love your neighbour instead of yourself" or "Love your neighbour and then if there is any time left over, love yourself." No! He says, "Love your neighbour as yourself." Sometimes, as women, I think we get the "love your neighbour" part really well, but we are not so good at the "love yourself" part.

Being a feminist and a person of faith allows me to live more consciously.[24] Now I want to look in more detail at the spiritual resources that help me as a woman with a chronic illness.

My friends rank high. The writings of Mary Hunt invite me to acknowledge that my friendships are a spiritual resource.[25] Among the gifts my friends give me is listening. Sometimes this means that they help me to become aware of how I am really feeling. I recall one friend, Dawn Rolke, who said to me, "Joan, some days do you feel so angry about having diabetes that you would like to just chuck your needles in the garbage?" Until she asked me that question, I did not even realize that I was angry. But once she asked, it became very clear to me just how angry I was. Her question gave me the permission I needed to feel what I was feeling.

A Bible story also gets me in touch with my anger. In the story of Jesus with the money-changers in the temple, Jesus becomes angry, very angry in the face of injustice (John 2:13–17). That gives me the permission that I need to feel angry about having diabetes. It is not fair and it does not make any sense. This story of Jesus' righteous anger has been freeing for me.

Another friend has been a spiritual resource for me by helping me to see that the greatest gift she could give me was that of accompaniment. She recognized that she could not "make it all better," even though there are many days in which I wish that someone could. What she can do is stand with me in my struggles. This particular friend gave me a card that said, "Until the world gets better, and even when it does, I want you to know that I accompany you on this painful journey you are on."

Another friend helped me to see that one of the gifts she could give me was some understanding about diabetes. She accepted it as her responsibility as my friend to learn about diabetes so that the onus would not have to be totally on me. The word she used was responsibility, not option. What an insight! I expend a great deal of energy trying to explain to others how diabetes affects me, energy that I sometimes need for myself.

Feminist music creates another spiritual resource that assists me in living with diabetes. One of those musicians is Arlene Mantle. Perhaps her most helpful words have been these: "We're building a new world, but we're living in the one that's here."[26] As a feminist and a person of faith, I feel called to help build a new world where justice forms a way of life for all people. While I work with others at building this new world, I see signs of hope.

At the same time, I also get discouraged because the pace of change crawls along so painfully slowly and sometimes not at all. When I feel that way, Arlene Mantle's words help me by injecting a note of realism along with the vision.

Another feminist musician who has helped me as a woman with diabetes is Judy Kaye. Sometimes I listen to her words, sometimes I read them and sometimes I find that they pop into my head just when I need them. "There's a river of birds in migration, a nation of women with wings."[27] My wish for all women with disabilities and chronic illnesses affirms that we would have wings, soaring above patriarchal assumptions, gliding over the seemingly insurmountable mountains of resistance to our stories, and comforting each other as a mother bird with her young.

Feminist community offers an important spiritual resource for me as well. That community first asked me to tell my story of living with a chronic illness. That community listened, really listened to me. Much healing comes in telling our stories and breaking the silence. Healing comes in being honest, and in refusing to pretend anymore, particularly in refusing to pretend that everything is okay when it is not.

While feminist community acts as an important spiritual resource, I have also been disappointed, at times, with feminist community. Sometimes people want to hear my story about living with diabetes, but do not want to hear what difference my diabetes makes in their lives.

Another spiritual resource that has been important to me is walking. I go for a walk by myself almost every day, which is for me a "holy" or "sacred" time. As I walk, I take the opportunity to get in touch with how I feel this day, sometimes taking stock of how I feel about living with diabetes.

That leads me to another spiritual resource that I have alluded to several times, namely the Bible or, more specifically, certain parts of the Bible. I already referred to the story of the woman from Cana, and the story of Jesus with the money-changers in the temple. Another biblical verse that resonates with me is Genesis 2:2 and 3, "And on the seventh day God finished [the work of creation] and ... God rested." Whether or not a person believes that God literally created the world in seven days, the words "God rested" can have significance for all of us. They certainly do for me. Like many other women, I often fall into the "superwoman" syndrome, trying to be all things to all people.[28] The passage from Genesis reminds me that even God took time for rest. If God can, surely I can too.

Since I became diabetic, rest is even more important than it used to be. However, another part of me wants to prove that I am as capable as anyone else, even though I live with diabetes. Therefore, I push myself, sometimes to the point of exhaustion and my health suffers. I am like the little engine in the children's story, *The Little Engine That Could*. Like that engine, I say to myself, "I think I can. I think I can." Sometimes, no matter how hard I try, I can't.

Another Bible passage that has been a wonderful resource for me comes from Isaiah's vision of a better world, of new heavens and a new earth. That passage along with many others in the Bible fill me with hope, that the world is changing, that there will one day come a time when justice reigns for all people, including those of us with disabilities.

> *For behold, I create new heavens and a new earth, and the former things shall not be remembered or come into mind. ... I will ... be glad in my people; no more shall be heard ... the sound of weeping and the cry of distress. ...*
>
> *The wolf and the lamb shall feed together, the lion shall eat straw like the ox; and dust shall be the serpent's food. They shall not hurt or destroy in all my holy mountain, says God.*
>
> (Isaiah 65:17, 19, 25)

Living with diabetes is not easy. People with chronic illness or disability are often ignored in our society and get the message that we do not belong. However, it is still possible to live, to really live, in our society. For me, my feminism and my faith help me to cope and indeed to live a life full of passion and meaning and justice-making. Many spiritual resources assist me along the way. I heartily believe that as we continue to ask the hard questions, as we continue to work for change and as the Spirit continues to dance among us, there will come a time when justice for all will blossom.

God Doesn't Make Junk
Christine Neal *Speaks*

I was born with spastic cerebral palsy (CP) in my left arm and leg. My hand is floppy and I walk with a slight limp that gets worse with fatigue. I attended public elementary and high schools and have just completed my Bachelor of Science degree in Nutrition at the University of Saskatchewan.

I am one of those people who does not fit in anywhere. In some ways, my disability sets me apart from people without disabilities. I can never quite measure up to their standards of beauty and physical grace. On the other hand, because my disability is fairly mild and generally does not impede daily activities, I can not usually identify with most people with disabilities.

I do not remember thinking too much about my disability when I was a child. Because I was born with CP, my hand and foot were just parts of my body that I forgot about except during physical therapy sessions. I was a really happy child. I played all the usual kid games like swings, monkey bars, and hopscotch. I loved riding my bike and swimming in the pool. The kids in my class readily accepted me and, in some cases, stood up for me against others.

In grade 2, a boy in my class got into a fight with a kid who was calling me names.

However, there was one particular incident that I will never forget because it was the first time that I remember realizing that some people thought that my disability was bad. When I was eleven, my grade 6 class was getting ready to do the nativity scene for the school's Christmas pageant. I really wanted to play Mary who was, after all, the leading female role. I must say that I looked like a Mary with my long straight brown hair and sweet angelic face. But I ended up being in the choir of angels because my teacher thought that I would be uncomfortable walking across the stage with my limp (at that time, my legs were two different lengths and so my limp was very noticeable). My teacher came to this conclusion on her own. She never once asked me how I felt about things. Until she pointed it out, I never knew I had a limp and so, walking across that stage would not have bothered me. In reality, it would have made her feel uneasy to see a student of hers limp across that stage. But I did not come to that conclusion for many years. At the time, I was just very hurt and bewildered at my teacher's suggestion that I was not good enough to play Mary.

For the most part, my disability was not an issue during my childhood. Yes, kids were very curious about my hand and asked me questions all the time and there were a few ugly name-calling incidents. However, I was in high school before my disability really affected my relationships with peers.

During my early and middle teen years, I struggled to be accepted by my peers especially boys. But, for reasons that I could not understand, most guys did not like me. They did not even want to be friends with me, let alone be my boyfriend. I always felt that they distanced themselves from me. As I grew older and tried to verbalize this feeling, my family and friends told me I was being paranoid and so I believed them. It was not their fault; they loved and accepted me for who I was and they could not see that there were some people who could not do that. I became very depressed during those years as I blamed myself for my inability to find a boyfriend. I thought that I was ugly and had a boring personality. In fact, I had convinced myself that I was unlovable.

My self-esteem was at an all-time low but it was several years before I was able to link my low self-esteem to my CP and people's attitudes about it. It was not until I had a long talk with a good friend who also has a disability that I was able to understand that it was often other people's fears and ignorance that prevented them from becoming close to me. I know now that I was not imagining things—some people really were uncomfortable dealing with me and my disability.

I do not want to sound like I blame everyone I meet for my problems. Most people I meet are great and have no trouble accepting me. My family, friends, and professors treat me like just a regular person. Indeed, because my CP is so mild, I rarely am subjected to blatant shows of discrimination. I am treated courteously in restaurants and stores. People usually do not notice my disability when they first meet me and when they find out about it, most people take it in stride. But there are those people, usually men my own age, who are put off by it. The sudden shifts in body language and conversation let me know that they are not interested in knowing anything else about me. Past hurts and rejections have taught me that it is better not to care too much at the beginning of a relationship because I always get disappointed. I do not trust men to stick around because too many have left just when I thought things were getting good.

I have noticed that nobody says too much about the prejudice and discrimination that faces people with disabilities. It is not politically correct to admit that you are prejudiced against people with disabilities. It seems to be okay to pity them and give them charity but it is a big no-no to say that you do not like them even if that is the truth. The prejudice and discrimination against people with disabilities is such a silent phenomenon. I know that some of my friends have trouble understanding and accepting that I have experienced discrimination. A few people have even tried to convince me that it is "all in my head." I can understand how people may have difficulty understanding my situation. Because my CP is so mild and does not prevent me from doing the things I want to do, people often perceive me as a person without a disability, or they may forget that I have a disability. But this does not matter to those people who are prejudiced against people with disabilities. Once these people discover my disability, they do not want to know anything more about me. They have already formed a mental picture of me according to the stereotypes in their mind. I will not even try to guess what this picture looks like but I am sure it is not pretty.

I do not always think of myself as a person with a disability. You see, it is fairly easy for me to forget about my CP. I have lived with it my whole life and so it seems normal to me. In fact, I think it would be kind of strange to have hands that could do two different things at the same time. Sometimes, I am surprised when I catch a glimpse of myself in a store window because, in my mind, I do not walk with a limp. I usually become acutely aware of my CP and feel uncomfortable about it only in the presence of other people. Some people stare at me when I am exhausted and have allowed myself to limp or when I shift a glass into the crook of my left arm in order to shake hands with someone. I can understand their curiosity about my disability but when they do not ask me about it and just stare, I am left feeling somewhat like a specimen in a museum.

There are times when I would like to, at least for a little while, wish my CP away. It can be really annoying when I am doing activities that require speed or grace because my affected side can slow me down and make me clumsy. My disability can also be a hindrance when I first meet people. So, at times, I strive to "pass" for an able-bodied person. Although I am aware that I want to surround myself with people who accept and love me totally, sometimes I just do not want to go through the hassle of explaining my disability to everyone I meet. Also, in some situations, I prefer to avoid prejudice than to confront it.

I get my strength to deal with the frustrations of having a disability from several sources. My family and a few close friends have been a constant source of support. They understand how my disability has affected my life. They do not ignore my CP but neither do they focus on it. They know that my disability and the impact it has on my life make up a small part of me.

My faith has also given me strength and peace throughout my life. It comforts me to know that God loves everyone unconditionally. My disability is seen by society as a physical flaw but I do not believe that God sees it that way. I think that saying "God doesn't make junk" is very true. To God, each thing in creation is beautiful because of its uniqueness. Anyway, with God, the spiritual side of a person counts a thousand times more than his or her body.

I also receive comfort from the knowledge that God is always with me and shares in my joys and sorrows. I am never alone when I face prejudice and discrimination. I can draw strength from God.

A Door to Hope

Elizabeth Richards (Liz) *Speaks*

About eight years ago I was in Banff, Alberta, with my family. I had been living with multiple sclerosis (MS) for about three years at that time. It was one of those slow days when moving was difficult and I was using two canes. We were going into a store where I had seen a picture that I liked. Just after we entered the store, a man looked at me with one of those looks that is halfway between pity and fear and said, "What happened to you?"

I was humiliated. I felt like I was damaged goods. I never really remembered just what I said to him. I know that I never went to look at the picture, I just turned around and left the store.

What I remember ever since that day was what I wished I had said. As soon as we left the store, I wished I had said, "Oh, a lot of really interesting things have happened to me. Would you like to hear about some?" Of course, now that I have such a great answer, no one has asked me that question. But I am ready!

That incident for me was a turning point in how I felt about myself as a person living with chronic disability. I realized then and there that I was going to have to do some thinking about who I was and what I was up to. If I did not, I was going to continue to be vulnerable to the humiliation of physical difference in a culture that idolizes the "body beautiful" and is deeply prejudiced against disability. Watch commercials. The body beautiful sparkles super clean and freshly scented, in terrific physical shape, often jogging or working out with weights, preferably quite slim, and usually young. Lots of us do not quite fit in! Some of us do not fit in at all. And there exists a strong, if subtle, social pressure to be as quiet and as invisible as possible if we have chronic illness or disability. In such a cultural context, it becomes terrifyingly possible to let ourselves be defined by others—and living with other people's definitions can eat away at self-esteem until suddenly, having internalized the social taboos around disability, we find ourselves depressed or even in despair. I have spent some time there. It is no fun.

I began reflecting on what hope and new life meant for me.

At first, I tried the "keep smiling" route. It worked a lot of the time. I denied the pain of the losses. But that pain became unbearable. It made me so lonely and sad to keep pretending that I did not care that my life was completely changed. The pain of loss is frightening and for a while I was scared to let it out into the open. But pain of grief comes out somehow, and I know I was pretty hard on my family and friends during those years. I was particularly hard on people I thought were whining or giving into discouragement. It finally became clear to me that I had to grieve the loss of who I had been before MS if I was going to find out who and what I was with MS. I made a deal with myself to tell myself and one other person each day how I really felt. If I was sad because I could not do something that had once been important, then I said so. Sometimes I cried a little. Sometimes I cried a lot! If I was frustrated, I said so. If I was angry because the world is not fair, I said so—to myself and to one other person, once every day. Then it was all right for the rest of the day to keep smiling and trying to find the positive side of things. I continue with that promise to name my feelings and situation honestly at least once a day to myself and to someone else. The habit has helped to ensure that I do not slip into the social expectation that I should silence my own life.

Denying pain was not a very good way to find life-giving hope. But I have found pain, acknowledged carefully and honestly, to be a reliable door into hope. I have come to understand that learning to live with MS is like learning to live after someone you loved dies. Admitting the grief, asking the questions of why … why me … why MS … why, why, why? Talking about it, expressing the pain that comes with loss of health and changed lifestyle creates the first step towards living a new life—a life, full and interesting, filled with many good things. A new life becomes possible as we replace the question of "why" with the question of "how?"

For me, hope is believing and expecting that my life has meaning, that I will grow and learn and have fun and love and be loved. It is believing and expecting that my life will be full and interesting, regardless of my physical ability or my health. It is the profound awareness that my body, just as it is, is "a temple of the Holy Spirit within [me], which [I] have from God (1 Corinthians 6:19)" and that as such I am a precious part of creation.

So I began my journey into a new and full life, a life where indeed "lots of really interesting things have happened to me!" A life with MS.

Probably because I am fascinated by metaphors, I began to look for metaphors that could help me live into hope and wholeness. I would like to share some of the metaphors for living with MS that I have found give me hope and help me to live even in really dark times.

We speak of people living in the fast lane. Such an expression makes us think of such exciting things: maybe work that involves travel, or meeting important people, or being an important person, or making important decisions. People who we say live in the fast lane are surely the movers and shakers. They have fun and contribute. They are busy people with a purpose. They generate money; they are valuable to the economy. Pretty heady stuff! Actually not many people live in what we call the fast lane. We just think that there must be lots and our culture tells us that we should try to find ourselves there to be successful. Fast lane has an attraction hard to put into words. Some of us know that from highway driving experience. I know I do not have the only heavy foot on the road.

Nothing prepares us to consider that we may find ourselves in the slow lane, or moving along in the parking lane. When I began to think of myself as moving along in the parking lane, or on some days as pulling over onto the shoulder of the road and just stopping, I saw the world around me quite differently. I was much more able to appreciate the beauty in nature: a sunrise, the wind in the clouds, flowers, snowflakes (in season!), the feel of the sun on my face, the sound of rain on the ground. The slow lane is not so bad. In fact, I now much prefer the sights and sounds and beauty of the slow lane and I often pull over onto the shoulder and just watch the world go by for a bit. I know now that I can be quite comfortable, life can be full and have tremendous meaning away from the pressure of striving to find the fast lane.

Changing the metaphor from fast-lane thinking and expectations to slow-lane/park-lane thinking and expectations gives me life. It is a great life in the slow lane.

Another metaphor came to me during a time when I was having a particularly long and frustrating attack. I was spending a lot of time lying on the chesterfield, on the bed, and in the reclining chair at home. I very much wanted to be out doing things. I was a student at the time; I was frustrated at having to miss classes and my pile of undone assignments was building up at an alarming rate. I was sick of resting. I was very sick of resting. I was listening to music when I got to thinking about the music score. I even got a piece of music and looked at it. Right there, in several places, as large and important as any of the notes and chords, were rests—some of them short, some of them long, but all very important to the sound of the music.

It was an "aha" experience. If in the busyness of notes following one another in music, rests held importance, then in the busyness of our world, maybe it was important for some people to be resting; some people whose job in that moment's scheme of things is to be representing the human condition at rest. Now I love to listen for the rests in music. I know that they have to be there. And I do not resent my own rest times which I still need to take. They have become for me a precious oasis of solitude and quiet.

A third metaphor also came out of my listening to music and thinking about it. I noticed that some instruments, cymbals for instance, are rarely played. But when they play, they make all the difference. The piece of music would not sound the same without them. During really quiet times, when it is hard for me to do things, I like to think of the cymbals waiting to be played—just waiting—not anxious—just waiting to be played. Cymbals are just as real when they are waiting in the hands of a percussionist as they are at the moment they are played. Other instruments, too, play only a few lines here and there in a piece of orchestra music. But they need to be there; the music would not sound the same if the people who played those instruments did not show up for a performance. I found that instead of thinking of myself as a violin or guitar or some busy instrument, I would be a cymbal or a tuba, meant only to play once in a while, but absolutely necessary for the orchestration that is life.

A particularly precious and helpful metaphor came to me while I was shopping one day. I love to watch those little crystal animals and flowers that rotate on mirror shelves in expensive china shops. One day when I was really having trouble moving, I saw a crystal snail. It spoke to me immediately. There it was! A snail, self-contained with house shell, intended in real life to very, very slowly be about its business. This crystal one was so sparkly and beautiful. It became for me a metaphor of the beauty and purpose of slow things, of slow life, of solitary life in the midst of the vast movements of lake or ocean, or world. If there are snails, then it must be all right to be slow and beautiful and alone much of the time. It has been a very helpful metaphor for me. In my first life, I was probably a deer or an antelope! This major change in the metaphors that give meaning in my life makes a profound difference to me.

Other metaphors help me: rat-race has been replaced by garden; I have replaced dance with poetry and so on. Finding life-giving metaphors offers one way of finding meaning for myself, my life and the realities of the world I live in. All of us, every single one of us has the capacity to find the meaning in our lives. Each of us will use a different path, a different way, a different door. For me, finding new metaphors helps me to understand myself as a holy part of creation.

Other things have also been part of my quest for hope and wholeness in the midst of broken body and broken world. An important part of my understanding of myself has to do with my need to be friend and to know friends. In the first years after I was diagnosed, I needed to try to stay in contact with my friends. Some could not accept disability or chronic illness and they slipped away. My presence was too frightening, too real for them. They did not want to confront the notion that my body (and therefore potentially their's too) could be out of control. Bodies, after all in our society, are supposed to be in continual and strenuous control. We are told that we need to control our weight, our beauty, our sensual drives, our body functions, our aging, and, ultimately, our dying.

I have begun to realize that the fear of loss of control and the fear of death are at least two of the roots of prejudice against people with disabilities or chronic illness. I have also come to believe that building friendships across the boundaries of physical and mental disability is a political act. By that I mean that friendships that can truly accommodate disability fly in the face of the attempt of our society to objectify persons with disabilities. People with disabilities can be controlled and the myth of eternal youth and wellness can go on without reality check as long as we are seen as objects. We may be objects of pity, of charity, of honour (consider the "special" language, e.g. "special" needs) or of disease classification. As long as we remain objects, our society can tolerate our presence. However, should we become real, live people with interests, opinions, needs, desires, emotions, or expectations, then society beware! I became committed to finding ways to be a friend and have friends.

I also value contemplation of the world of nature. Over the

years of living with disability and the unpredictable nature of multiple sclerosis, it has become increasingly significant for me to understand myself more deeply as a part of the natural world. To know that I am an integral part of the same creation where deer run and jump so surely over fences and ditches, where puppies play and horses quietly feed in the evening pasture, is to appreciate my own spark of life and to allow my life to enter the wider life around me. I do not need to be able to run to feel the thrill of watching a hawk circle high and then drop to catch a meal. It is not necessary for me to walk in order for me to feel the wonder and freedom of movement as a flock of geese flies over. When the dog runs to catch a stick, I am part of the motion as I watch. I do not need to have personal muscle coordination to appreciate the delicate work of a spider spinning a web. I can be moved deep within by the song of a bird or the sound of the wind in the trees. Increasingly, I treasure entering into the creation of which I am a part. To the extent that I am able, I find that I am also blessed with the passion to work towards healing for the planet.

I also understand the door into hope and meaning to be found through religious experience. All of the world religions offer stories, metaphors, and traditions that help people find a way into hope and wholeness, regardless of circumstances. For me, religious tradition has been very helpful. However, I am well aware that others have experienced judgement and slight when they have tried to question their experience of chronic illness or disability in light of religion. I continue to believe that when spiritual questions are asked honestly—the questions of hope, of meaning, the questions of how to live and find life—when those questions are truly asked, they will be truly answered at some point in any one of the world religions. We are all on a spiritual quest. It is human to seek out how we are connected to one another and with the forces of creation. For me, learning to live into wholeness has meant that I needed to explore more deeply my faith tradition.

Religion is like a treasure castle; it takes a lot of time to explore all the passages and rooms, the beauty and the pain, the light and the shadows. Since living with MS, time is something I have quite a bit of! I find that religious experience can be profoundly meaningful when I take time to explore and trust. As I struggle with, and continue to re-examine, my understanding of the presence of God in my life, I return time and again to Dorthee Soelle's book *Suffering*. I particularly like her discussion of acceptance in the midst of suffering: "The prerequisite for acceptance is a deeper love for reality, a love that avoids placing conditions on reality."[29]

Every one of us has within us the ability to find meaning in our lives. We will each find meaning and hope differently, but it is a gift that is ours to find and keep. Each of us is infinitely precious, not because of what we do or do not do, not because of ability or loss of ability, but because we hold within us the flame of spirit that makes us human. However we name that human spirit breath, as long as we live we hold that precious treasure for the whole world. The world needs us: our ideas, our love, our friendship, our very presence. The world is suffering and hurting right now. The world needs now as never before, the voice of those who are learning how to live in hope in the midst of pain. It is important not only for ourselves but to the world that we hold onto the precious treasure that is our life and that we find the way to live with hope in the midst of despair, with peace in the midst of struggle, with courage in the midst of fear.

We cannot do that alone. We cannot do that if we deny our pain and the pain of the world. But I have come to believe that when I give voice to my own experience, when I encourage others to do the same, the silence that has bound the lives of those who live with chronic illness and disability is broken and we can together claim our strength and wisdom. Together we will find the power to live with wholeness and to offer healing to our society and to all creation.

Faith, Fury, and Fibromyalgia
Elinor Johns *Speaks*

Barbara Elliott was a dear friend of mine, and I honour her in participating in this writing project. In this process, she has continued to call forth my energy to do what at many moments I felt I could not do—or did not want to do!! Writing is a resource for me when I am willing to do it. For me, to write is to pray—to be heard and to hear.

I bring to this project my experience of living with a condition called fibromyalgia. Fibromyalgia syndrome is a chronic, often disabling medical condition, characterized by widespread body pain, specific tender pressure points, fatigue, and sleep disorders. It is often accompanied by many other problems such as general stiffness, irritable bowel, headaches, irritable bladder, and cognitive impairments. I carry this "diagnosis" as lightly as possible and live with it with varying degrees of faith, fury, and frustration. In 1988 I was diagnosed with chronic fatigue syndrome. I had experienced these symptoms for a number of years previously. These symptoms and their severity vary from person to person, from day to day or week to week. This illness has taught me that I can no longer take many things for granted! Fibromyalgia is a relatively recent name for the specific set of symptoms often diagnosed earlier as chronic fatigue syndrome. Chronic fatigue is a part of the fibromyalgia syndrome. The medical name for the diagnosis does not change the bodily experiences of it.

Much can be said about the experience of living with disability or chronic illness, and about the spiritual resources for and of this experience. What I am learning from this provides part of the foundation for the work I now do. My life is also richly coloured by other experiences—among them growing up in rural Manitoba, training and working in diaconal ministry, being married to Rob Johns (Rob died in 1986 within a few months of being diagnosed with cancer), and being mother to Stephen, born in 1974, and Carol and Sheila, born in 1977.

I offer a collage of reflections, most of which engage the issue of relationship. How does living with disability affect/change/ enhance my relationship with myself? How does living with chronic illness affect/change/enhance my relationship with others? How does living with disability or chronic illness affect/change/ enhance my relationship with the Holy? The variety of writing styles represent the various ways I have explored these questions. I invite you to enter the readings in a variety of ways. Find ways to make them a resource for your own reflection. Use them as a beginning point for your own journal writing. Play with reading them aloud.

Community (or Feminist Theological Communion)

Separated by
    miles
        disabilities
            callings
                months

and the phone would ring
at my home or yours

Barb,
    I knew
    that you knew
    I was here.

Living with a disability

requires

a lot of

ABILITY

How refreshed I felt recently when the C.G.I.T. Purpose, from my youth, bubbled to the surface of my consciousness.

As a Canadian Girl in Training
under the leadership of Jesus,
it is my purpose to
>   cherish health,
>   seek truth,
>   know God,
>   serve others,
and thus with his help
become the girl God would have me be.

Cherish health—it was like hearing it for the first time. How wonderful it is that at that time I was given the permission I need now to be attentive to my health, to healing, to wholeness.

Cherish health—called now to be in my body/mind/spirit whatever the state of my ease or dis-ease.

For me, living with fibromyalgia has meant that I am always living in pain, sometimes acute, sometimes easier to ignore. This means that often, too often, I regard my body as an enemy, as a part of me that betrays me.

I have been fortunate to have Joan Turner as my massage therapist/counsellor.[30]

> For me massage therapy has provided
>> a place of sanctuary
>> a place for safe touch
>>> for relieving, reliving, releasing,
>>> acknowledging and honouring the pain
>> a place for befriending my body
>>> again and again
>> a place for exploring the patterns
>>> and the passages
>> a place for giving up
>>> and taking hold
>> a place for being heard
>>> and for hearing myself
>> a place of healing
>>> Sanctuary
>>>> Praise Be.

After contemplation: John 5:1–9, a passage offered to me at a retreat.

> *After this, Jesus went to Jerusalem for a religious festival. Near the Sheep Gate in Jerusalem there is a pool with four porches; in Hebrew it is called Bethzatha (or Bethesda). A large crowd of sick people were lying on the porches—the blind, the lame, and the paralysed. A man was there who had been sick for thirty-eight years. Jesus saw him lying there, and he knew that the man had been sick for such a long time; so he asked him, "Do you want to get well?"*
>
> *The sick man answered, "Sir, I don't have anyone here to put me in the pool when the water is stirred up; while I am trying to get in, somebody else gets there first."*

Jesus said to him, "Get up, pick up your mat, and walk." Immediately the man got well; he picked up his mat and started walking.

Broken
Exploding
Despairing
    by the pool
        of
            Disappointment
            Discouragement
            Disbelief

                muddy
                stagnant
                cold
Jesus comes
        questions
        acknowledges
        responds

This pool is not for you.
I will show you another way.
Your faith, such as it is
            Broken
            Exploding
            Despairing
has moved me.

Go with strength and energy.

Journal entry after a massage

Rib Cage

Like a caged one
Throwing herself against the ribs
(bones become bars)
Until she is bruised, exhausted.

Today she will rest
tend the wounds
allow the pain to flow
from deep within.

She learns to befriend the cage
and to find the doors.

Accompaniment

Misery is optional.
She who speaks thus
speaks her truth.
Be with her awhile.

Misery is misery.
She who speaks thus
speaks her truth.
Be with her awhile.
Be with her awhile.

Journal entry

Sometimes I grieve the losses.

The Shadow cast over my life

Picking all the flowers
—of my gifts
—of my spirit
—of my connections

leaving me

Empty handed
Clenched fisted
Desolate

A car accident when I was four or five years old may have contributed to the body/mind/spirit dis-ease I live with now. Alone in the back seat of a moving car, I accidentally opened the door and tumbled out onto the gravel highway. The physical shock was compounded by the immediate realization that the adults in the front seat did not know what had happened, and so, for an eternity of seconds, I ran after the car. One day, during a massage, I relived this terror. Then I wrote:

I am a running sore.

>
> Come, I will hold you,
> enfold you.
> I will lovingly
> staunch the blood
> dress the wound
> mend the heart
> before you go out to play.

I am a running soul.

>
> Come, I will hold you,
> enfold you.
> I will lovingly
> dress you
> in your body
> firm & snug & clean
> Before you go out to work.

I am a running shoe.
Fired by adrenalin
and gravel
I cannot catch them
Worn thin.

>
> Come, I will hold you,
> enfold you,
> honour you
> and then let you go,
> replace you
> sturdy and new
> and
> of your heart's desire.

Restoring your soul.

Self-Esteem: A Family Affair

A particularly useful resource for me in living with disability are the Affirmation Ovals written by Jean Illsley Clarke.[31] Originally designed to give language to parents, as parents learn the messages children need to hear first at particular development stages, and then for ever after, they are also a wonderful support to me as an adult who is knowing and growing!

Today, for instance, as I was working to deadline, and feeling inadequate and stuck, I flipped through the affirmations. These are the ones that spoke to me:

With thanks to Jean Illsley Clarke & Connie Dawson.[32]

Claiming Community

To be a part of community is vital to me. How do I live out my experience of living with chronic illness in the midst of community? And in the midst of my experience of chronic illness, how do I discover, recognize, and participate in community? This has been for me a most persistent challenge.

I have learned that I can know what and who I need in this regard. Here are some of the questions I have asked myself that have helped me find some answers.

- Do I need many people or a few?
- Do I need to play or to pray?
  —to sing or share dreams
  —to learn to laugh
  —or cry?
- Do I need to be with people who share similar challenges or different ones?
- Do I need a new community?
- Do I need community within my geographic area or away from it?
- Do I need transportation to create community or telephone time or postage or a modem?
- How can I claim what I need?

Discovering Community

In different times and in different ways I seek and find and lose and seek and find again, this community, this connection:

with a friend who shares similar challenges.
with a family member or friend across the miles.
with a health-care provider who can listen, accept, comfort, confront.

in a walk or a phone conversation with a friend or co-worker.
in a support group for people with fibromyalgia.
in a group like the women's singing group I have joined, where I can enjoy my ability to sing and enjoy music.
sometimes in the reading of another's experience or listening to a radio interview.
hugging a son or daughter.
alone, at a retreat centre, with a friend at home who has agreed or offered to care for my children.
in a women's circle. I am blessed to be part of a small interfaith women's circle that has been very life-giving for me. We gather to talk, to laugh, to listen, to exclaim, to discern, to complain, to question, to make meaning. Sometimes we talk about dreams or—or colours emerge on paper—or tears on tissue! The forms may change—and the focus—and the energy becomes synergy and the circle continues.

Journal entry

STAY UNDERWHELMED

I have learned to value my dreams as a spiritual resource, and I share them regularly with a small group of friends.

My aunt, Gertrude Staples, lived with a physical disability. Following a car accident in which her spinal cord was severed, she could no longer walk. I was 12 years old. She returned to her career as a school teacher one year later. A formative person in my life and the life of my family, she died in 1989 in her eightieth year.

In the midst of this writing project, Aunt Gert came alive to me in a dream:

> I am going to visit her in a small plain room in a hospital. I am aware that I have not seen her for quite a while. When I open the door she recognizes me and then turns to me with an expression of sheer rage.
>
> And then I am returning to see her, and again I am feeling that it has been too long. I open the door, and I do not see her at all, only a dry stick-like figure on the floor, and I think she is dead. I kneel down to touch her.
>
> And then she springs to life, and she is wheeling down the corridor, talking animatedly to me as I walk beside her. We are moving towards a school blackboard at the end of the hall. There are numbers on the blackboard and people waiting to be taught.

I awaken startled by the intensity of the rage: her rage and yes, mine. I am burdened. Do I still feel the guilt that I did not visit her often enough? I recognize the dry death-like experience of loneliness. I marvel at the life-giving magic of touch. I am encouraged by the possibility of moving forward to new life and purpose.

This dream became a rich source of comfort, challenge, truth telling, connection, hope.

Walking the Mother Path

Carol Rose is a Jewish writer, teacher, spiritual counsellor in Winnipeg, Manitoba. She is also a woman who experiences a disability, and she is my friend.

She has produced a set of Walking the Motherpath cards: "a set of poetry and visuals designed to use the Biblical mothers as models for growth and transformation."

The cards can be used in a variety of ways. For example, what I need today in my confusion, is the focus in the face of Rachel. What I need today in my aloneness, is the trusting embrace of Ruth and Naomi.

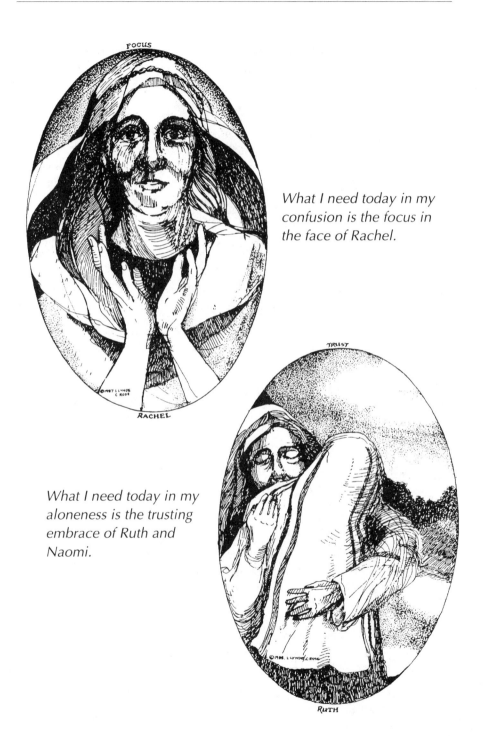

What I need today in my confusion is the focus in the face of Rachel.

What I need today in my aloneness is the trusting embrace of Ruth and Naomi.

The music of women singer songwriters has become my hymnody, my connection, my praise, my freedom, my faith, my reflection, my passion. Among these are:

- Ann Mortifee "Born to Live"
- Connie Kaldor "Wood River" and "Strength, Love, Laughter"
- Karen Howe "Circle of Difference"

"Born to Live" by Ann Mortifee

We were born to live not just survive
though the road be long and the river wide
though the seasons change and the willows bend
though some dreams break some others mend

We were born to give and born to take
to win and lose and celebrate
we were born to know and born to muse
to unfold our hearts, take a chance and choose

We were born to love though we feel the thorn
when a ship sets sail to return no more
though a door be closed and we feel the pain
to chance it all and to love again
We were born to reach, to seek what's true
to surrender all, to make each day new
we were born to laugh and born to cry
to rejoice and grieve, just to be alive

We were born to hope and to know despair
and to stand alone when there is no one near
we were born to trust and to understand
that in every heart there's an outstretched hand

We were born to love, to be right and wrong
to be false and true, to be weak and strong
we were born to live, to break down the wall
and to know that life is to taste it all.[33]

Once when I was sick and troubled, I was reading Psalm 23. In a effort to make it "real," I put it into my own words:

> The One who created is also
>   my friend
>   letting me rest
>   quenching my thirst
>   giving me new strength
>   showing me the way.
>
> Though beset by doubts
>   and fears
>   pain
>   loneliness
>   still I feel accepted.
>
> I am showered with
>   beautiful gifts of
>   love
>   caring
>   encouragement
>
> I am confident
> I know I will always
>   be welcomed.

I wrote this visualization based on Psalm 23 for a healing retreat.[34]

VISUALIZATION March 12, 1988
Relax the Body
Find a position that is relaxing and comfortable to you.

If you are sitting, keep your back straight, your legs uncrossed, and your hands unclasped.

Close your eyes.

Focus on your awareness of your breathing.

Breathe slowly and deeply.

Be aware of the sensation of the air (rich with oxygen) entering your nostrils—and then

leaving your nostrils—

Breathe deeply—I'll give you a minute to do this.

Relax the mind
As your body relaxes, I'd like you to let go of those thoughts and voices that you may still be carrying with you. In order to do this, you might see before you a huge tent, filled with people, objects, feelings.

Concentrate on this tent.

Suddenly a gust of wind blows through and sweeps the tent free of all the clutter. Your mind, like the tent, becomes uncluttered.

Continue to breathe—again being aware

of your inhaling—

exhaling.

The Journey
Now I'd invite you to go on a journey (or you may choose not to go).

I'd like you to visualize yourself going slowly down a hill into a valley.

Look around you at the surrounding hills—are they steep or gently rolling?

Be aware of the warm sunshine at your back.

Notice that it is quiet—only the occasional crunch of twigs— and the sound of your own gentle breathing.

You come onto the flats of the valley and notice the river there—a quiet bend in that river, joined by a natural bubbling spring. Take in that scene.

[Pause]

You notice a small boat tied to the edge—it seems to invite you to go for a row. You get in and gently row around the bend in the river.

You notice sheep grazing in the pasture alongside.

You row the boat to the other shore and when you alight, you are aware that a mentor or special friend (your wise woman) is coming to join you. She is loving and caring and wise.

You greet each other. You talk.

You spend some very important time together *speaking* of that which is most on your heart—

and *listening* to the answering voice of the wise one. Do this until you hear my voice again.

[Pause about 5 minutes]

And now you prepare to part. Thank your friend, your mentor, your wise woman for support and suggestions—receive a blessing, and bid farewell.

Then return to the boat and row around the bend, back to the river's edge.

Alight from the boat, and move across the flats, up the hillside, hearing the crunch of twigs, being aware of your quiet breathing.

Move back to your usual waking reality. Return now, relaxed, refreshed, and energized. When you are ready, open your eyes and stretch your body.

To close, I would like to tell you about one of the resources that I have found most helpful. It is the book: *Life is Goodbye Life is Hello; Grieving Well Through All Kinds of Loss.* Alla Renee Bozarth is an Episcopalian priest/therapist.

She closes her chapter on sickness with a vision. "More and more I believe that a perfect universe is one which absorbs a great deal of imperfection. Completeness contains incompleteness. Wholeness includes a whole lot of unwholeness." When one views life in this way, judgements, recriminations, guilt, self-hatred, and blame do not dominate. Acceptance of things as they are enlarges vision and opens a person to new fullness of life. It allows ambiguity, letting us and our loved one's "to be neither here nor there, but in between ... and to learn from this."[35]

I would also add that imperfection absorbs a great deal of perfection. Incompleteness contains completeness. Unwholeness includes a whole lot of wholeness.

This vision is echoed in a conversation I recall with another wise woman. In 1988, my children and I arrived in Calgary for Christmas to be with my sister, Beth, her husband Richard and their three children. One by one, we came down with stomach flu. I apologized. Beth said: "A healthy family takes sickness in stride."

Let's envision the kind of society that, like a healthy family, incorporates disability and chronic illness into its well-being.

A Woman's Urge to Dream

Sharon Davis *Speaks*

I am sitting here, in front of my computer, with that blank, stony, strange look that appears to be incomprehension. Many people have this look when they sit in front of their computers. In my case, it is not incomprehension, but a feeling of fear as comprehension dawns. I have been sitting here for hours on end over the past few months, and have finally acknowledged that I do not want to write these words. To share thoughts, I have to go back; I have to remember and I have to re-feel things that I have put in some unending place in my soul and heart, nevermore to be brought out. But they can never stay there. They can never just be part of the past. If we are to be on the journey of life, if we are to continue to move and grow and have being and become, we have to take out those experiences of life over and over again. We do that so we do not become stagnant or dull or ignorant or once again, too fearful to enjoy what is rightfully ours to enjoy in faith: the gift of life from a warm, loving, gracious, and humorous creator, in whose image we are all created.

At my desk, right in front of my very eyes sits a wonderful picture of Barbara J. Elliott. There are no tubes attached, no oxygen, just that delightful smile. When my eyes wander to it, I hear her chuckle and words that say, "Oh Sharon, just sit down and write!"

To start, I share a poem written by Rosemary Doran, as found in *Images of Ourselves*.

> God created humankind in God's image.
> To know ourselves, then, is to know something about God.
> What can I know about God from myself?
> I am human, I am woman.
>
> I know joy and tenderness,
>   patience and empathy,
>   long-suffering and endurance,
>   creativity and nurturing.
> Are these not also found in God?
>
> I am human, I am woman.
> I know pain physical and emotional—
>   and outrage
>   and frustration
>   and, sometimes, despair.
> Does God not also know these?
> ...
> When I look at you, I am looking for God's image in you.
> When you look at me, do you see that image in me?
> God grant that I may reflect something of the one who brought me into being.[36]

That is why I must remember and share and write and get that strange look off my face.

As I write this, I am 48 years old. I deal with a disease called, by doctors, "the Old People's Disease," as it usually strikes persons well past middle age. For 28 years, doctors have said to me, "How come you have this? Usually only 'old' people have it," as if I chose to have degenerative osteoarthritis, and as if "old" people want to claim territorial rights to it!

I had never considered myself disabled, although it was more than a little apparent that I could not walk very far without problems. My breathing was the pits, and life in general was on a bit of a down swing. Thus in my early twenties, I learned that there were things called arthritis and asthma that could affect every facet of my being in ways previously unknown to me. Shortly after this, I was also diagnosed as hypertensive, and down the years, diagnosed with diabetes and glaucoma, all of which helped in creating a good, healthy ulcer. I do not say this for pity, but simply to let you know from where I speak. I have long since learned that pity is neither desired nor helpful. Compassion and respect are very welcomed and cherished.

So while my birth certificate says 48, many doctors convinced me I was old. Parts of my body definitely feel and function as if they were much older. On my bad days, my soul too, feels significantly "on in years."

These diseases that physically challenge my being mean I no longer can walk unaided. Most days I use one cane, but on bad days two. If things are really troublesome, I use my wheelchair. I now have a scooter, thanks to my mom and my dad, who so lovingly have cared for me even after their lives in this place called earth have ended. My scooter changed my life in ways I could not have imagined. The year I got it was the first year in many that I was able to go shopping in the stores for Christmas gifts. Signs of hope in life are found in new mechanical technologies, as well as medical advances.

Pain dwells as a constant in my life. The constancy wears more than the pain itself. Many moments of pure unadulterated anger, frustration, and tears come. Some days I resort to pain medication, but usually I try "pain management," because the anti-inflammatory medication causes my stomach and ulcer to go into jet speed. The stiffness, swelling, and inflammation in my affected joints, (toes, ankles, knees, fingers, wrists, shoulders, neck, and back—God bless good hips!) keep me from many things. Two major changes are the ability to work only part-time, and the decreasing ability to play the piano as I want to, and used to.

These two things affect not only my functioning, but the core of my being. Music, and particularly piano playing, has been an integral part of my ministry for 25 years, not to mention soothing the savage beast in my soul.

The first time I allowed myself to use my wheelchair, a friend said she would take me to the mall. I needed to find a pair of winter boots. Off we went. On arriving at the shoe store, we noticed three other customers and one clerk. We looked at boots and waited. As we watched, we realized that the other customers were not in buying mode that day, but the clerk seemed to be running around in circles anyway. It soon became apparent that he was avoiding us. When there was one women left, he literally went and tried to hide behind her. Finally, no one remained in the store but my friend, me, and my wheelchair. He walked over to us, looked at my friend and said, "Can I help you?"

"No," she said, "but you can help my friend here!"

"We don't have anything for her," said the clerk, and turned around and walked away. I cried that day in fear, in confusion, in humiliation, and in despair. This man is not alone. He represents, symbolically, the majority of people in our world, who, for the most part are unaware of what they really see, and fearful of what they think they see.

Diet controls my diabetes. Being diet-controlled means I do not use pills or insulin injections, so have no way to balance things. If I unknowingly eat something detrimental, I have no way of counteracting. Diabetes also means pricking the old finger four times a day, about three times a week.

The hypertension and ulcer mean medication every day, but, as long as stress is limited, create minimal difficulty. I do need to say that dealing with arthritis, asthma, diabetes, and glaucoma produce a certain amount of stress! But I truly could deal with that stress, if it were not for the attitude of so many in our society.

One of the things that does bring hope and joy to my life is people who are aware and caring. A friend in our community of faith plays the organ for church services. Every Friday, Marion comes to practise. Many of those days, she brings a treat for people at the church to eat. She always brings two plates—one for everyone else, and one for me. At the annual meeting of Saskatchewan Conference, she came in with a big container full of snack treats for those of us with diet limitations, because she was not sure that at the coffee corners there would be anything we could have. The food itself is nice, but the understanding, the thoughtfulness, the caring, the time and energy she takes are the nicest of all. Still the arthritis and asthma put limits on exercise, meaning I have to work hard at the minimum control I do have to keep from having to be on insulin.

Asthma produces a few trips to the hospital, but regular doses of three medications (some of them steroids) keep that to a minimum. I find comfort in going to the emergency ward of the hospital I live close to, and having the nurse look up and say, "Oh, I remember you; down to Room One."

One of the things that Barb and I talked about a great deal was that no one, including doctors, believed you knew anything about your body or your illness. This proved a bigger problem for Barb, as she did know more about her illness than just about any doctor. For me, hope in life arrived with Dr. Pam and Dr. Joanne. Pam first suggested to me that I needed to work part-time. She did not push or harass me. She simply outlined the issues and all the implications, then left it up to me. It was two years before I would go to her office in tears and tell her I thought it was time. Pam comforted and understood; Pam haggled and pushed the incredibly insensitive, uncaring, unknowing, and I might add, rather ignorant, insurance company I would deal with over disability pension rights. Pam, and now Joanne, have restored my faith (somewhat) in the medical profession. They have shown me that they trust my judgement, my understanding of my diseases, and my intelligence. And I believe they have come to understand that, just as they want me as healthy as possible, I also want health. I am grateful for these two women, after spending years of being ignored, unbelieved, and, in a real sense, abused by the medical system.

As of yet, I do not use drops for the glaucoma. This will

produce some problems when that day arrives because the medication does not agree with people living with asthma. Up to now it has meant eye checks every six months. This means having someone to drive me, as the four drops per eye mean that sight is limited.

In spite of everything, it continues to be the arthritis that inflicts the most visible problems. On a beautiful sunny prairie day, I had just had my hair cut, which is always a morale booster. My friend and I went back to the van to leave for home. As we were "buckling up," a man walked over to the window on my side, and stuck his head inside. In a very threatening voice he told me I should not be parked in the disabled parking spot. I kept trying to assure him that I was quite within my rights to park there. I physically kept straining to keep my face more than a few inches from his as he kept coming, surprisingly, through the window. "You've been parked here for three hours! [it had been an hour and a half] I drive the Kinsman Van, and I couldn't park here. You have no right to be here at all. You're not incapacitated enough to use disabled parking!" I tried, once more to assure him that I was incapacitated and that I had the proper licence on my vehicle. "So what?" he said, "anybody can get those." I cried again that day, but with far different feelings. Although somewhat afraid of him, I was angry, and no longer prepared to silently slink away out of his life. Who did he think he was to tell me how incapacitated I was? Why should I feel obliged to try and prove it to him? Who was he to imply disabled plates were a sham and I was a part of that sham? Who did he think he was that he could invade my van with his face and abuse me? We were in Melville at the time, and drove to the police station, only to find that they do not work on weekends. You have to contact them in Yorkton. So we went back to where we had come from, found out who the gentleman (I use that term loosely) was, and came home. I wrote a letter (a darn good letter) and sent it off to the Mayor of Melville. While I have not received the response I hoped for, I have received indications that action was being taken.

A young carpet cleaner entered the house the other day. He

mentioned that he had seen the scooter, and asked why I used it. When I told him, he said, "Well, what's wrong with you anyways?" Having explained, he said "Oh, so you don't have a serious bone disease or anything like that?" Sometimes I get caught off guard and slip. I almost apologized for being a disappointment to him.

Many issues surround being disabled. Many emotions are hard to describe. I have struggled with, I have enveloped myself with, and I have rejoiced in the mix of emotions: anger, confusion, fear, lack of self-worth, celebration, joy, and humour. Yes indeed, lots of humour. After all, "Sarah laughed," and God invented the belly button and facial hair. What more do we need?

As I look over the years, I have had, and continue to have, many sources of hope, of inspiration, of love, of support, of understanding, and of just plain good life.

My mom was, and will always be to me, a most remarkable, wonderful, warm and wise woman, and one of my greatest sources of hope, inspiration, love, and support. In her life, she coped with an incredible number of physical problems. I learned from her. Our heritage of faith taught us to "suffer gladly," and quietly I might add. We were taught to "bear our burdens and our crosses." Alone. That was what the Bible told us, or so people thought. My mom was like that, or so I thought—until I thought more deeply. That happened when I was beginning to deal with my own life issues. She did not just "bear" her burdens, she dealt with them, and out of those experiences she became the remarkable, wonderful, warm, and wise woman that she was. Because of that, she helped me to begin to deal with my issues. I bear one regret about my mom. She did not live quite long enough for me to be smart enough to tell her all these things. She knew I loved her, and held her in deep wonder and respect, but it would have been good to talk about our diabetes, our eye problems, and our faith. Don't wait too long. Life simply does not go on forever. People out there ready to listen and share.

A few years ago I realized that I could no longer live alone. Some mornings getting out of bed presents a problem. Some days getting into the tub creates an issue, not to mention getting out.

There are times when getting out of a chair, off the toilet, tying my shoelaces, dressing, doing up zippers and buttons, getting in and out of vehicles, opening and closing doors, or just looking at myself in the mirror, exasperates me. Occasionally I am holding a glass, (or a plate of stew), and away it goes. It usually spills on the rug, because mopping the linoleum or wiping the table would be just too easy. I needed help. But you have to have the right kind of help, a very special kind of help. You have to have someone who understands, who does not get mad even when you drop your plate of stew all over the newly cleaned rug. It has to be someone who knows when to get up and help without being asked and who knows when to ask. That person needs to be someone who does not mind the rather unglorious job of helping you off the toilet, still making you feel worthy, respected, cared for, and fun to be with.

I have a friend like that. Her husband died two months before my mom. She happened to work with Barb Elliott, so Barb decided we should talk. And we did. About two years after both of our losses, I knew I needed help. The following year she decided she had lived alone long enough. We talked. I discovered that her diabetic father had suffered a major stroke when she was four years old. Her entire life had been lived with someone who was disabled. She knew what it was about. How about a boarder, Jackie? Well, let's give it a try. We have been trying for four years now, and we are still very good friends.

One of the best moments of my life was meeting Barb Elliott. That happened in 1970 when I was interviewed by the committee that would say yes or no to my becoming designated as a Deaconess in The United Church of Canada. I remember her at that interview, and I remember her following me out of the room, walking down the hall with me and saying, "I think we're really going to get along quite fine." Barb brought, and always will, so much to my being in the way of friendship, laughter, analysis, questioning, and more questioning, and great wisdom. Her most special gift was through our shared involvement in instigating what now is the Christian Feminist Network in Saskatchewan, and *The*

Unbeaten Path newsletter (currently named *Unbeaten Paths*).

After one of the early winters she spent in Berkeley, California, we ate supper together talking about her experiences there. She wanted to be able to talk with an ongoing group about the things she had discovered, learned, read, and experienced. That week Katharine Anderson and I were in her office, and we decided there was nothing to stop us from creating just such a group. And create we did! We each chose one other person, and these six ultimately became the group. The other members were Marilyn Perry, Marion Thompson, and Dorothy Logan. We met once a month for several years. In the second year of our meeting, we became intensely concerned that women in general should have the kind of opportunity we did: an opportunity to have some kind of network, to talk about the kinds of things we talked about, for organized support and caring, a way in which we could share learnings that we believed were important to women, and means to affect the world we lived in. We talked. Then Barb got to work. Out of this came an entirely new perspective of life for me about what it meant to be a woman, and ultimately a disabled woman in such a "health-expected" world.

Other sources of hope and strength to me have been music, playing and singing, and reading. In 1981, a group of women gathered at St. Andrew's College in Saskatoon. It turned out to be one of the most intensive, supportive learning experiences in my life, and I suspect in the lives of others. Dorothy Logan and I collaborated on a song out of our experiences. Dorothy wrote the words and I the music. Over the years, the meaning of this piece has changed for me, as my life has changed. With permission from Dorothy, I share with you the words, and hope they will become meaningful to you as well.

WOMANSURGE WOMAN URGE

Thank you for love, for holding me, seeing my worth.
Thank you for rage, for sharing my death and urging my birth.
Woman surging in many streams,
Woman crying in many storms.

Thank you for giving me woman's new power to live once again.
Strong hearts together, freeing each other,
from prisons dark and old.
New dreams and visions, stirring and boiling,
and cracking those walls of cold.
Thank you for struggle, for grief that is healing my loss and my pain
Thank you for giving me woman's new power to live once again.[37]

We so often repress our creative gifts and feel that we "just couldn't do that." It is not true. In fact, being creative offers a wonderful way of dealing with all those feelings that we do not know what to do with. It allows us to identify what they are, name them, own them. It helps others become aware. It gives knowledge. In fact, creating is a responsibility and an act of faith, that we cannot deny if we are to enable some change.

Another major source of hope and vision for me has been my faith and the Bible. In an article called "Good News For Modern Woman," Lois Klempa writes about how women have not readily seen the good news of Jesus' revolutionary treatment of women in the Bible. She says:

> Jesus went out of his way to make it abundantly clear that his teaching, unlike that of other rabbis, was meant for women as well as men. Search as you will, nowhere in any of the gospels will you find a word that would give any indication that Jesus believed women to be inferior or subordinate. No wonder women flocked to hear him. 'Is it any wonder,' as Dorothy Sayers says in 'Are Women Human', that women 'were first at the cradle and last at the cross? They had never known a man like this Man there has never been such another.'[38]

Jesus' anger at the injustice in the temple in Mark, chapter 11, has always been incredibly significant to me as is the woman who was determined to have her child healed and would not be told what 'her place' was. The woman who made Jesus listen to her and change his mind in Matthew 15 gives me hope and courage. In Genesis we find Leah who was considered a poor catch as a wife because of impaired vision. She, too, reacted with anger and continues to affirm for me the belief that we can all change and grow. These women affirm for me that it is good and right for me to acknowledge, to own and to deal with all my feelings whatever they may be.

In Galatians 3, we hear that everyone is equal. I know that means that as a woman, as a disabled woman, I have as much worth as all on this earth.

In Genesis, I hear and believe that I am made in the image of God. What better can there be? All of this, and much more allows me to celebrate the words of JoAnne Walter.

> There is no part of me unlovely
> Not the anger, or the pain, or the sorrow,
> Not this physical being others see as me.
> These are the things that draw me deeper
> into womanhood
> where I am called to be.
> It is the place where we have met,
> To grieve and laugh and celebrate.[39]

The United Church tells me that "we are not alone, we live in God's world." This God who "has created and is creating."[40] is my reality, and my dream and my vision.

I tell one more story from my life that holds up one of those rays for me. I went into a craft store using my wheelchair, selected an article, and proceeded to the counter to pay for it. A clerk waited on a customer. I pulled up, and shortly after, another woman stood behind me, waiting her turn for the attention of the clerk. The clerk stood in front of me and to my right. As she finished with her customer, she leaned past me to the woman behind me, and said, "Can I help you?"

"No," said the woman politely, "you can help this customer who was here before me."

The clerk rudely said, "What do you want?" I handed her my article along with the money to pay. She rang it up, proceeded to slide it over the counter to me (just in case what I had was catching, I presume), and watched as it all slipped to the floor. As she did this, she again leaned towards the woman behind me. "Can I help you now?"

"Not just yet,'" said the woman pleasantly. She turned to me, smiled and said, "If it would be helpful, you could just wheel ahead and I can pick up your belongings." Then she waited as I wheeled ahead.

I turned and said, "Thank you so very much."

"You're welcome," said this wonderful human being. "Now" she said as she leaned over towards the clerk, "you can help me."

One more ray has been a gift to me from Native Spirituality. Dreams are important in Native Spirituality. Dreamcatchers, as symbols, have become very meaningful to me in the recent past. In Ojibwa culture, dreamcatchers hang by the cradleboard of an infant or child. The round hoop represents the circle of life or eternity.

The dreamcatcher was placed near the sleeping child's head to capture both good and bad dreams. The bad dreams were caught in the webbing and when the sun rose were burned off in the sunlight. The good dreams trickled down into the feathers to be saved and dreamed again.

Another story tells that the good dreams passed through the centre of the dreamcatcher to be dreamed by the sleeping child. The bad dreams became tangled in the webbing and feathers to be burned off in the morning sun. Some say the dreamcatcher was given either as a wedding gift or to newborn children so that all the dreams for the future would be good ones.[41]

I, too, have dreams. I dream that there will be a day when I will be in that unknown entity called new life. In that unknown entity I will be able to look into my mom's eyes and say, "Thank you for your incredible wisdom, patience, gentleness, your love and your enjoyment of life." I dream that in that same entity, I will look up to Barb and say, "I did write, and for that I thank you." I dream that in that same entity, I will look out on God's earth, and see that all is well, that people are treated as images of this great Creator, and I will thank Her too.

Enduring Towards Justice

Charlotte Caron *Speaks*

I was a sickly child. My self-image formed around being sickly. In first grade I received an award for having done well at school despite missing so many days. Mostly I went on will power. Digestive problems, sinus infections, respiratory infections, and aching legs plagued me, and I looked pale with dark lines under my eyes. Chronic exhaustion was my companion. Growing up in a rural area at that time meant limited availability of medical expertise. I occasionally went to the hospital with digestive problems or pneumonia. My mother fed me milk soup and toast when I was sick.

This self-image of one who was sickly continued. As a young adult, I lived through painful bouts diagnosed as gout and varying forms of arthritis. Menstruation cycled irregularly and agonizingly. Environmental and food allergies increased, as did digestive problems. Skin lesions, hives, and flaky skin were common. In middle adulthood, a diagnosis of asthma was added. Finally I was working with a medical doctor who believed that something was really wrong with me. She did every test she could think of and sent me to several specialists. We did a variety of food elimination tests, some of which seemed mildly helpful, others of which made no difference. Then I did a yeast and mould elimination. Within three days many signs of asthma were cleared up. In ten days, what I had always called "the ball of lead" in my stomach had dissolved. As time went on, the leg pains and violent muscle cramps stopped. My menstrual periods became more regular. The dark lines disappeared from under my eyes, and my eyes opened in the morning instead of resisting the day with swelling, stinging, and irritation. I stopped running into walls and doorways when I walked. Depression and thoughts of suicide lessened. While these symptoms did not disappear forever, their intensity and constant presence shifted.

Candidiasis

I began a regimen of symptom control for candidiasis, the condition caused by an overgrowth of yeast in the digestive tract. Normally, the yeast organisms in the intestines feed off dead or dying tissue. When they become pathogenic, they feed off living tissue and release toxins into the body through holes they poke in the cell membranes of the intestines and other warm mucous membranes. These toxins can then irritate any other system in the body. Candidiasis, environmental illness, fibromyalgia and chronic fatigue syndrome have similar symptoms. Different medical doctors and practitioners of alternative health care often diagnose the same person differently. All are immune system disorders, which means that symptoms are diffuse and appear in one or several body systems (for me, the respiratory, muscular, reproductive, neurological, gastro-intestinal systems). I have chosen to speak specifically about Candidiasis although I have been given different diagnoses from different practitioners.

Because Candidiasis is an immune system problem it is triggered by a variety of irritants and has multi-ranging symptoms. Avoidance of irritants and actions to strengthen the immune system are the primary means of control. For me, this means avoiding a wide range of foods such as dairy products, sugars and sweeteners, vinegars, yeast, mushrooms, alcohol, fruit, tofu, corn, tea, and condiments. I do not tolerate certain chemicals well such as gasoline (I cannot go to self-serve gas stations), diesel fuel, natural gas, printer's ink (so I do not read the daily newspaper), tobacco smoke, wood smoke (no campfires or fireplaces), cleaning fluids, perfumes and cosmetics, paint, ammonia fumes, insect repellents, or air fresheners. Any mouldy or dusty environment creates problems. Spring with leaf mould and blossoms is difficult. I need to avoid animals.

Generally, if I avoid all the things I need to avoid, do all the things I need to do (eat well, sleep a lot, and exercise regularly), I appear physically healthy. In fact, I have some days of feeling well. Other days pain and unpredictability reign. My life is strongly affected by the reality of this yeast-complex/environmental illness syndrome. I still have a self-image tied up with being sickly.

Spiritual questions emerge out of that self-image. For example, Christian theology understands all people as made in the image of God. Does the image and, therefore, the nature of God include disability and sickliness or chronic illness? Christians have tended to stress the perfection of God, and, therefore, the idea of God incorporating chronic illness and disability is theologically challenging.[42] Am I in the image of God if I am chronically ill? Am I perfect? Is God perfect? Can God, in fact, be disabled? Is all creation good as the Bible suggests?

Unpredictability

One of the problems with chronic illness is its unpredictability. I never know when the good and bad days will come or how the bad days will affect me. Immune system disorders attack all of the body's systems. I never know whether it will hit my muscles today, or my respiratory system, my menstrual system, my digestive system, my joints, or somewhere else. My neurological system is also out of kilter so some days my legs and brain refuse to connect. Then my feet become unworthy of trust. I find days when my legs do not work properly because of nerve or muscle problems most difficult. I assume mobility and walk a lot. Usually walking creates well-being for me and it does help my digestive and respiratory problems. But on the days when I hurt all over and my legs do not work properly, when I fall or run into walls and doorways, I have to admit that my body functions differently from many other people's bodies.

Living in an uncertain state wears on the spirit. Jean Blomquist describes becoming chronically ill by saying, "As days passed, I wrestled with the reality of being chronically ill—sometimes believing it, other times thinking it couldn't be. Then came the monotony of living with illness each day."[43] In many ways one's world narrows with the advent of chronic illness. For me, staying home often feels easier than going out with the social and physical risks involved. Kathy Charmaz notes that "Staying home is a major strategy for managing illness ... By staying home ill people can jettison both public self-presentation and the preparation it entails."[44]

Preparing the special food I need to eat demands time and energy. I require organization and discipline to keep at the tiresome tasks involved in staying well. As well, I work for a living. Unlike many people with chronic illnesses and disabilities, I do have a level of income through my work that allows me to buy the relatively expensive foods I need and to pay for certain energy-consuming activities such having my house cleaned.

Control and Agency

I went through a phase of trying to get control of this illness. When I look back I can see that it was part of a bargaining phase of grief about my body. I joined groups, took courses, wrote, talked to people, read and researched, did everything I could think of to understand what was going on with my body, hoping that if I understood, surely I could have some control over it. But what I came most to understand is that chronic illness does not go away. I can never really control it despite my valiant efforts. I find this depressing. Even now, some days I accept the realities of my life; other days I rage and grieve.

I struggle with not having as much freedom as I would like for being spontaneous. I have to think and plan ahead. Will there be anything at this function for me to eat or should I take my own food with me? Will there be smoking? Will there be animals, perfumes, flowers ... ? Will I be able to move if I sit for a long time? What do I need to do tomorrow that will be affected by today's choices?

Another issue related to control arises for those of us with invisible disabilities. It relates to when and whether to tell people. Kathy Charmaz helpfully distinguishes between protective disclosing and spontaneous disclosing. Protective disclosing occurs when the person with the chronic illness plans to tell people, gives them information, and eliminates as much of the risk in telling as possible by choosing time and place. Spontaneous disclosure happens when there is little control over the coming out and often includes expression of raw feelings and exposure of oneself.[45] Both occur. Sometimes telling people that I have limits in what I am able to do flows easily. Sometimes it grates painfully because of the external circumstances, or because of how I feel on a particular day.

Like many groups of people who live with discrimination in North American society (such as gay and lesbian people, Jewish people or people of First Nations descent who are mistaken for members of the dominant culture), people with invisible disabilities and chronic illnesses sometimes choose to closet their differences. This silence means choosing to pay a private cost rather than a public cost for telling the truth about our lives. When we speak out, we often have to deal with other people's emotions and reactions as well as educating them about what is needed. Many people simply do not think about the consequences to me of their responses when I tell them about my illness.

From my perspective, control over one's life is a spiritual issue. Some streams of Christian theology emphasize submission to God's will and letting go of control so that one may be a selfless instrument of God's service in the world. Liberation and feminist theologies, however, focus on the concept of agency. Agency means that people should be able to participate in the decisions that affect their lives, should be able to act to affect their destinies, or, in other words, should be able to exert some control over the state of their being. Loss of control over one's body and one's days features large as part of chronic illness. This loss provokes deep questions of how to retain agency, how to have any control over one's life, and what appropriate control is.

Legitimacy

All of us need validation to have strong self-esteem and well-being. Yet commonly, others de-legitimize our lives by discounting our claims, accusing us of exaggeration or of wanting attention. A relative urges me to have a fresh dinner roll. An old friend greets me in a supper line at a pot luck, "Are you still on that weird diet kick? I thought you would be over it by now."

We all have to eat to live, but the social culture of eating gives meaning to our eating habits. Although my disability is invisible in some circumstances, it is visible at meal time. The culture in which I live focuses on eating as entertainment. Pot luck suppers and lunches after meetings are the usual fare for events at work, in the feminist community, and in the church. Almost every gathering has food. Not to share the food provided is often interpreted as an affront, as refusing hospitality. People providing food are often hurt or embarrassed when I cannot eat what they offer.

In North America food and comfort are linked. Like many women, when I am feeling emotionally deprived or overwhelmed by circumstances beyond my control, I want to eat and I develop tremendous cravings for the most toxic of foods.

I have discovered that many people do not think having a dysfunction related to eating constitutes a "real" problem. I have been told frequently that I am not really chronically ill; everyone has to restrict their eating or go onto diets sometimes. Being believed and given legitimacy become important in the spiritual desire to have a meaningful life and a sense of well-being.

For many years I annoyed doctors. Because environmentally based illnesses frequently produce diffuse symptoms, no one found what caused my health problems. In childhood, I lived with the contradictions. My parents were distressed by my frequent and sometimes severe illnesses. Often they would take me to the doctor and be told by the medical system that there was nothing wrong with me, or that I likely would be better soon. This pattern persisted through much of adulthood even after diagnosis.

A moment of grace occurred recently when I visited my neurologist. I had been going through tests for most of a year to try to determine the cause of my frequent tripping and aching legs. After a final round of checking the nerve sheaths in my brain, he said, "Well, the good news is that you don't have a brain tumour, and it is not likely MS, but there is clearly something wrong with you and it is hard on my ego not to be able to solve this problem!" How refreshing it was to have him name the situation as his inability to solve a problem rather than saying there was nothing wrong with me! I was given respect and legitimacy.

Suffering

There is no easy way to live comfortably with pain. On the days when my body aches and exhaustion overwhelms me in ways that sleep cannot fix, I get discouraged. My friend, Myra, who has fibromyalgia commented, "People always say that your emotional state and all the things you have to work out in your life influence your body's well-being, but I know it is my bodily state that influences my emotions." I agree with her. When my body works, my emotions are much broader and healthier than on the days when my body constrains my energy. On those days my emotional spectrum narrows, and I turn my frustration inward. One day I wrote in my journal:

> I came home and sat down and I started to cry. For days my body has been in pain and in the state of refusal where it feels like muscles have no tone, no strength, no capacity, where feet will not lift high enough to walk, where hands can barely grasp a pen, where every motion has to be thought out and made deliberately. Why wouldn't I just cry? I get so angry, frustrated, and disappointed with my body. I don't cope well with pain. I try to

ignore or trivialize it. If you live with it constantly, pain becomes normal; you can only complain and demand nurture if it flares to acute. I want to sleep. I don't want to be touched when I hurt this much. I just hurt.

Certain strains of Christian theology have suggested that God gives pain and suffering to provide meaning and that we simply must search for that meaning. New Age philosophies stress that we choose our illnesses and disabilities because we have something to work out in this life. Both of these formulae blame the victim. Neither provides satisfactory answers. Susan Wendell is much more helpful when she states, "having experienced a crisis of meaning in my body, I can no longer assume that even powerful bodily experiences are psychologically or spiritually meaningful. ... With chronic pain, I must remind myself over and over again that pain is meaningless ... "[46] I find it constructive to believe that there is no inherent meaning in suffering, chronic pain, chronic illness, or conditions of the body that are disabling. They simply exist as part of the diversity of creation. Not everything has meaning.

Endurance

One day as I was talking to women at a Candida group, I became aware of the strength of our will power. We talked about sometimes barely being able to move, not knowing how we can put one foot in front of the other to keep walking. I have been this way much of my life so do not think about the fact that it takes me ten times the effort to do things as it does for others. It is hard for me to recognize that there are people who never realize they have stayed at work past the critical time and are not sure if they can make it home, who have never thought about sitting down on the sidewalk and crying because it feels impossible to take another step, whose feet do not drag in the snow because lifting feet in snow is too hard, people who greet new days with eagerness instead of only getting up by sheer will.

Eleanor Haney claims endurance as a spiritual resource. She says that endurance shows that the human spirit is tough, that it will hang on and not say no. Endurance "enables people to lead complex and meaningful lives in the midst of incredibly dehumanizing conditions." She contends that theological and ethical literature often ignores endurance, focusing on what we should do in situations rather than on the question "how much longer can I hold on doing what I have to do?" She suggests that hanging on shows "a self exercising responsibility, a self of often tremendous moral courage."[47]

Endurance seems like an important spiritual resource for people with chronic illnesses and disabilities. Endurance displays moral strength and spiritual courage in the boring, exhausting, and uncertain times.

Anger and Justice

Anger forms another potential spiritual resource for people with chronic illness and disabilities. Our society prevents many people from participation by erecting barriers. Social and political structures exclude or marginalize some people. In this context, anger appropriately motivates for change.

Women in our society do not have many role models for healthy anger. Most white, middle-class, North American women learn patterns of cultural adaptation that encourage us to become nice rather than angry. We live as nice women and adjust our lives to fit in. But this often means holding a great storehouse of rage just below the surface. This submerging of anger is a societal rather than an individual problem. It is not the natural state of women's being. But like a toxic spill in the environment, it is hard for us to avoid breathing it in, absorbing it, and experiencing its mutating effects.

Disabled women who express their anger are especially at risk if they are dependent on attendants, caregivers, families, and friends. We cannot afford to make enemies; we may need those people to keep us alive. So, often we repress anger or turn it on ourselves. Women commonly blame themselves, asking "What did I do to cause this?" Sometimes women's anger is viewed as a symptom of our illness.

Anger can, however, be the motivator to create change. Anger can be a powerful agent in moving towards justice. Justice requires addressing the real world inequalities that exist, and changing social relations so that all people have access to the resources they need to participate freely and fully in the community. Action to change structures that perpetuate the violence of sexism, heterosexism, able-body bias, racism, and classism is essential for those who profess a liberationist faith and desire a just world. Both attitudinal and functional barriers need to be addressed.

From my perspective, structures and relationships that embody justice create the foundation for spirituality.

Inclusive Communities

Fortunately I am able to gather for dinner once a month with a group of women who live with chronic illnesses. Like a lot of friends, we talk about what has been happening in our lives. Here, the news is likely that one has been in hospital, another has finally gotten confirmation that her company will pay disability insurance and we celebrate that now she will not have to return to a job she cannot cope with physically, another has had more rounds of medical tests. Ideas emerge for coping with pain, for alternative therapies, for which doctors will be supportive of people living with fibromyalgia, chronic fatigue syndrome, and other disorders with "vague and diffuse" symptoms. We grieve together the loss of relationships in our lives when people want us to be more healthy and vigorous than we are, we grieve the loss of identity that comes when someone is no longer able to be in the sphere of paid employment, we weep over the comments people make to tell us we cannot be sick when we look healthy, we laugh as we invent the things we wish we had said when someone has not understood the realities of our lives. Mostly we are reassured that our lives are as we experience them.

Sometimes I do not have enough energy to take initiatives in relationships. I am grateful for friends who do initiate contact with me and for a women's group that meets in my home where I have some control over the environment. I need safe places to talk

with people about what my life is like and I need those with whom
I share intimacy to take seriously the struggles I face. I need
people who help to eliminate the risks and who provide some
sense of solidarity. I also need people close to me who are not
critical if I decide to go off my health-care program occasionally
(even though I know there will be consequences of doing that)
and who will let me decide when to go off.

Chronic illness and the regimens of health affect intimate
relationships. For example, the Candida Research and Information
Foundation estimate that less than 25 percent of intimate
relationships and marriages survive where the woman has serious
candida.[48] When the daily routines of making a living, exercising,
resting, and maintenance consume all of one's energy, relationships
tend to suffer.

How can we have truly inclusive communities that enable all
people to live as richly and fully as possible? This feels like a very
difficult question at a pragmatic level. Churches, other spiritual
communities, and feminist communities claim a desire to be
inclusive communities where people of varying life circumstances
feel welcome. But, in fact, our practices frequently falter on
inclusivity.

For example, the practice of communion in the Christian
church includes sharing bread and wine. How can all be included
in this activity? Do we simply say that people should participate in
whatever ways they can? While I cannot eat the bread and drink
the wine, I can hear the words and see the bread being broken
and wine being poured. A deaf colleague may not hear the words,
but can taste the elements, while a blind friend cannot see the
action but may be able to taste and hear. Is this sufficient? Some
communities of which I am a part offer rice cakes for those who
cannot have bread, but bread is the key element and the rice
cakes are clearly for those impaired from eating bread through
chronic conditions or eating disorders. If we desire to be a
community, why not use rice cakes? Why not be more creative in
our liturgies and create new norms of who is central? To create
inclusive communities challenges assumptions. Yet we can choose

to know the limitations and strengths of those with whom we share in community, to listen to those who are frequently excluded from full and free participation, and then to work very hard to make room for all. I believe that no one loses in an inclusive community. We all gain by participating together.

Diversity

Inclusive communities address the reality of diversity. This is difficult in a North American society that claims homogeneity as one of its highest values. If we are to be viewed positively, we are to be white, middle- to upper-class, preferably married with a couple of children, able-bodied, employed in the market economy, mobile, educated, male, and living in a democratic country. Clearly, most of the world do not fit those norms. We are diverse. White skin is a minority hue in the rainbow of humanity. Poverty is the norm for most of the world. Marriage is not possible or desirable for many. Our physical and mental disabilities and chronic illnesses mean many of us do not fit the norm. Not all people have access to market employment. And not all of us are male!

Diversity enhances spirituality. When we encounter different beliefs, practices, body shapes and functions, and life circumstances, we add richness to our understandings of life, our searches for meaning, and our perceptions of the Holy. Creativity blossoms: together we invent ways to live in a disabling society. We offer different perspectives on ethical decisions and social issues, on living with loss and limits, and on facing fear and life-threatening situations. People with disabilities and chronic illnesses are essential to spiritual communities if the communities are to be inclusive and just. All of us need, in our diverse circumstances, to be seen and to speak for ourselves—to participate meaningfully in whatever ways we are able—in the wholeness of society. Silencing the voices/realities of disabled and chronically ill people means losses for all of society.

My spirituality opens up questions and explores ideas, possibilities, and visions. In community, we explore the questions and gain new insights that help us in our daily living. In our longings, we find small signs of hope. As we live with integrity and tell the truth about our lives, we can discover paths to more just and compassionate living. We can grow to enjoy the diversity of our lives and live into the creativity that will allow us to be in truly safe and inclusive communities.

A Vision Is Not an Easy Answer
Jayne Whyte *Speaks*

Visions must be created in community. I cannot create a vision by myself. As I climb back up to hope after yet another plummet to the deepest of despair, all my strength goes into survival. Little energy remains for my goals and dreams, or for a vision of justice, equality, and life for women who live with disabilities.

I am alive, when not long ago I was planning to be dead. I was supported by friends who love me and I didn't overdose. I was cautioned by the weekend in 1987 when I took more than enough pills and had more than enough time before I was found. God sent me back. I don't have memories of great white lights and loving presence, only of my rage. God had seen my pain and despair, and my body was still alive. I hated the God who had rejected me. I hated the people who said, "God must have a purpose for you." And most of all, I hated myself.

I yelled at Jesus, "I don't understand. Why did you agree to resurrection? I understand about descending into hell. I just don't understand the coming alive again. How could you go back to a father who killed you?"

In 1987, I had just recalled memories of sexual abuse; rather than betray a father I loved, I decided to die. God sent me back to face the torture of my flashbacks, to experience the horror of my broken and bleeding body, my life poured out. "Do this in remembrance of me" took on a whole new meaning.

Regaining the memories explained so many things: the recurring depressions I had had since the age of fifteen, the difficulties I had finding and keeping jobs, the fear and confusion around my roles as daughter, wife, mother. A diagnosis of multiple personality (dis)order helped to explain the wide mood swings, the disorientation that overcame me, the disconnected internal and external sensations. I began the process of finding, hearing, and accepting my internal community, re-membering myself.

I found one part whose main job was to be good and love Jesus and go to church. She loved me so much that she did not reveal herself until many of the angry, sad, and hurting parts had been heard and were healing. Her love was deep enough, patient enough that she waited; she worried that caring about her might hinder the stories and release of other parts like Angry-Sad, Fighting, and the Little Kids. She told us her name is Christian, and she understands herself as God at work in and through my life. Christian has changed because she knows a more complete story instead of a child's Bible picture books; I have changed because I recognize that core of love and hope and goodness in me.

I am grateful for the community of personalities that share my body, and the community of friends who surround my life. I am still angry at God, still angry that parents could so betray a trust so many times. Angry that my mother could tell me, "If you don't love your parents, God can't love you." Angry that I couldn't find my dad that night in 1987 when I went to death to look for him. I long for my mother to validate my memories, to confess her own sorrow, to make reconciliation possible.

A community of acceptance and compassion allows us to face and to feel all of ourselves. A collective wisdom among shared joy and pain, past and present, enables us to dream and work together towards a future that includes sufficiency of material goods, healing what can be repaired, and thriving as well as surviving. That is my vision of what justice and equality could mean for all people who have been hurt by the individual and collective errors and omissions of our less-than-perfect society. I know there are no easy answers.

Symbols of Abuse and Healing:
A Reflection on Healing as Trust and Action

When we are suffering, we ask, "Why?" Is there any meaning or purpose? Where can we look for life? Where can we look for hope? How can we take control in an impossible situation? Does God have anything to offer? Does the Christ who was crucified have anything to say to people who suffer as the result of abuse?

This chapter is being written by a feminist Christian with ambivalence about the symbols and structures of Christianity. Despite doubts and despair, trusting a God who loves me, a Christ who suffered, and an ever-present Comforter have been integral to my journey. I want to share my struggle to reframe the cross, snakes, and other horrors into symbols of healing for myself and for others who have experienced physical, emotional, and sexual abuse.

Note that when I speak of healing, I am using the widest definition: well-being that can transcend or transform physical or emotional suffering. For some of us, healing may mean getting well, that is, reducing or eliminating the trauma and physical symptoms. For many of us, healing represents a process in our lives and our relationships where we face the physical and psychological evidence. We look at it, we decide to live as fully as we can, and we move on.

Healing as both trust and action may or may not fit into traditional patterns. The Christian symbol of the cross as suffering and redemption may or may not be helpful, but it cannot be ignored. I no longer wear a cross as a public symbol of my faith because it offends some individuals. I have walked with women whose suffering has been justified through corruption of the cross. Their emotional, physical, and sexual sacrifice was perpetrated by authorities who used the name and symbols of God and

Christianity to increase and to warrant their power. Survivors of ritual abuse may see the cross as an instrument of torture without connotations of salvation, atonement, and resurrection.

Within and beyond the church, many people deal with personal experiences of crucifixion, waiting, and survival. Lent and Easter are hard times for me. The hope of new life in the Christian story and the budding of nature can contrast sharply with personal fear and despair.

Memories and fear of torture and suffering persist in the souls of people who have endured neglect, abuse, and danger. Snakes are a recurring nightmare for several friends who have been abused. The phallic symbolism is only part of the picture.

How can we reframe the power, the shame, the guilt, the fear? In my experience, healing begins when we face what we fear and learn to handle it. We cannot change the physical and emotional reality of the past. However, we do not deserve to carry the responsibility for those who violated our trust—men, women, and institutions who abused their power—and our bodies and minds.

An illustration I have found useful in working with depressed and hurting people refers to the story of the bronze serpent on the staff of Moses (Numbers 21:4–9). I do not endorse a god who says, "You're complaining again; you deserve to be punished." But I suspect God got blamed because the Israelites camped in the migration path of snakes. The story points out that their energy was focused on destroying their neighbours and complaining about the rations.

We can identify with these people who are angry and discouraged. Listen to these wanderers in the desert: "Are we there yet?" "I'm tired of this journey." "How many more battles?" "When will food taste good again?" or "I'm so tired I could just lay down and die." So when they were bitten by the snake, some of the people did just that; they lay down and died.

The snake on Moses' staff has been perceived as foreshadowing the crucifixion of Jesus the Christ. What do the stories of the cross of Christ and the snakes wound around Moses' staff say to people who are facing the horror of violence in the present or in memories of their past?

How were the Israelite people healed in the wilderness? They looked at themselves and they looked for a cause for their suffering. They looked to their God. Each man, woman, and child was asked to look outside themselves. They looked at the object they feared the most as a method to regain health and power in their own lives. Or as the story says:

> The people came to Moses and said, 'We sinned when we spoke against the Lord and against you. Pray that the Lord will take the snakes away from us.' So Moses prayed for the people. The Lord said to Moses, 'Make a snake and put it up on a pole; anyone who is bitten can look at it and live.' So Moses made a bronze snake and put it up on a pole. Then ... anyone [who] was bitten by a snake and looked at the bronze snake ... lived.
>
> (Numbers 21:4–9, NIV)

Unfortunately, we may not be delivered from our suffering. But we can find tools to help us. Notice that the snakes kept on biting, but because the people's focus changed, they lived. All the people had a choice. They could refuse to look at the snake, just like we can choose to say, "I don't deserve to live" or "There's no use trying; I'm doomed." The people who could not lift their heads and look beyond themselves held onto their despair and died. People who looked at what was hurting them were healed. They were ready to look beyond themselves for health; their courage and faith were as important as the symbol of God's grace. The next paragraph of the biblical story begins, "The Israelites moved on ... "

In John's account of the conversation with Nicodemus, Jesus is quoted as saying,

> Just as Moses lifted up the snake in the desert, so the Child of Humanity must be lifted up, that everyone who believes in [me] may have eternal life.
>
> (John 3:15, NIV)

The verse that follows the reminder of the bronze serpent is a familiar John 3:16:

> *For God so loved the world that God gave God's own*
> *Child, that whoever believes in the Child of God should*
> *not perish but have eternal life.*

For God so loved the world ... that couldn't possibly mean me ... must be God loves you but not me ... or me but not you ... No, God's love and God's promises are for everyone! And how do we, individually and as community, claim this promised life?

People who experience low self-esteem are encouraged to make affirmations. For example, "I am a worthwhile, loveable, and capable person." We are encouraged to act as if we recognize our own value even when we feel inadequate. Sometimes the hardest task of the friend and therapist is to get people to even admit the shadow of a hope that they are loved and loveable. (I know; I've been there!)

Jesus affirms that his purpose is not to condemn the world but to save it. Some people may feel confused that Jesus continues from this triumphant affirmation of love to a discussion of judgement. But think about it. God gives us a choice to participate in our lives and healing. We can choose to believe we are condemned and hide or we can believe that we are healing, that our life can move on. Each of us can remember a time when we confronted a truth we did not want to face, a deed we did not want to remember.

The light is turned on, and we choose; we could shut our eyes and stay in the dark. A fireplace offers warmth and we choose to approach it or to stand apart shivering. If we are in pain because of sin, we can choose to talk clearly and listen honestly with the person who has wronged us or whom we have wronged. Each of us must examine the actions, words and attitudes that have been causing pain to us and to others. Past actions, words and attitudes continue to persecute us if we condemn ourselves. The alternative is to look at the bronze serpent. Or as Jesus says:

This is the verdict: Light has come into the world, but
[humans] loved darkness instead of light because their
deeds were evil. ... But whoever lives by the truth comes
into the light, so that it may be seen plainly that what he
[and she] has done has been done through God
(John 3:19, 21, NIV).

As a survivor whose mental illness is the result of childhood abuse, I am very concerned about the group of parents and professionals who have formed a foundation to accuse the victims of abuse and their therapists of False Memory Syndrome. The victims reveal the crimes, and the perpetrators choose to remain hidden. Those who refuse to walk in the truth are condemned already. For many women seeking help with their nightmares, the snakes on the doctor's cadeusus symbolize medical abuse of power; doctors and therapists from whom we seek help may deny our experience or urge us to get on with our lives without acknowledging our pain and offering us hope in our healing.

We seek help. Suffering throws our lives out of balance in our physical, emotional, social, and spiritual being. The snake bites us. The snake in ancient Hebrew thought was identified with sin, a symbol of saying "I know better than God about what I should eat and what I should do." In other traditions, the snake is a symbol of life energy and renewal; the snake symbolizes resurrection when it sheds its skin and goes on living in a new skin. This story of Israelite people in the desert exemplifies snakes as symbols of healing, deliverance from sin. (We just can't get away from that word—sin.)

We live in a sinful society. Too often the individual child, the individual woman, the person who has been persecuted assumes she is bad and deserves to be punished. Sin is the collective attitude of our society that rewards power, violence, betrayal of trust, lies, threats, and violation of persons.

We need to redefine the word "sin" as a societal concept. Sin does proliferate in our world. And people are affected by that sin. Discern that the sin that afflicts us may be the result of another person's or society's sin. Sin is revealed by a society that does not value persons, destroys creation, and uses power and privilege destructively. Think of it—abuse, violence, poverty, disrespect, lies, cheating, unjust accusations, unkind words—those are sins and they hurt people. Sin hurts people who are innocent as well as people who are guilty. And sin continues to cause suffering in our world, in our families, in ourselves.

The church has also been guilty of perpetrating and concealing violence, a shelter for men and women who do good works in public while destroying lives in private. Even when individual people acting in God's name have not had an active role in abuse, many church leaders have joined the accusers who blame the victims of abuse. Almost all of us know a woman who has been advised to return to her battering spouse. Teens and adults who seek help may be told to forgive those who persecute them. There are still civic and spiritual leaders who persecute people who threaten their reputations, reveal their secrets, and challenge the status quo. And people who have been further abused or dismissed under the sign of the cross cannot be blamed for fearing its power and persecution.

For the church to become a healing place, it must face its sins and the people that it has sacrificed. Not all the religious leaders agreed to Christ's crucifixion but that did not save Jesus from death. The cross is a sign of redemption because persecution and destruction were followed by resurrection and renewed hope.

People who are suffering may find comfort in the image of Christ as one who is suffering with them. "Jesus was crucified because of the sins of others" is a tool we can use to reassure people who have been abused that they do not deserve punishment even when it has been inflicted. Many victims can identify with a Saviour who would protect others by receiving the abuse and punishment instead of seeing his sisters and brothers hurt.

The story of the crucifixion is the story of manipulation, intrigue and betrayal of someone who did not deserve to suffer and die. We hear that Jesus went about doing good, healing and teaching, and challenging the status quo. People who speak out about abuse challenge society's self-concept as right and righteous. And we may draw courage from the Christ who came to love the world and was condemned to death by its civic and spiritual leaders.

People must look at themselves, accept their responsibility, and accept both the truth that they sinned (or were sinned against) and the truth that they are loved by and acceptable to God. Persons who have been abused can be healed by coming into these truths. However we cannot restore relationships and be reconciled with the ones who choose to stay in the lie: abusers who refuse to accept responsibility or refuse to acknowledge the abuse. We may still love them; we mourn that the closeness is broken when contacts consist of accusation, denial, or silence regarding our experience.

God and Jesus Christ continue to love us no matter what has happened to us or what we have done. But our Creator and Friend will not force anyone to look at the serpent on the pole or the love of God on the cross that can save and heal.

The view expressed here is that Jesus' death has meaning related to salvation. The way to salvation, that is, healing and well-being, is to look at the cross: to live with the flashbacks, the horrors, and the truth of the abuse that happened. Through looking at the truth, healing, salvation, and, potentially, reconciliation can happen. This is a different view from authors such as Joanne Carlson Brown and Rebecca Parker who contend that all atonement theology (theology that says the cross was for salvation) raises the question of God as a Divine child abuser.[49] Both of these perspectives push for major re-visioning of traditional theologies of sin, salvation, and the cross.

We need to be reminded that although we may not have any choice about experiencing disability and pain, we do have a choice about where we focus our attention, how we respond, where we look for life. The snake-bitten Israelites chose whether or not they looked at the healing serpent on the staff of Moses.

The God I know leaves each of us free to choose. Yet, often we seem to have no choice; we face circumstances that seem unfair.

We face illness, pain, loss. The truth is that God does not condemn us. God loves us whether we are looking at images of hope and healing or keeping our eyes turned inward in our despair. The Israelites in the desert were saved by the faith that let them look at the source of their healing: the love and protection and purpose of God.

God sees no intrinsic value in pain and suffering. Because people, individually and collectively, make choices to betray trust, misuse power, violate relationships, sin and suffering are part of this life that individuals cannot always understand or explain. But when we are suffering, we may draw courage from the suffering and courage of others including Christ. Like the snake-bitten Israelites, we choose where we look for hope and healing. To me, the empty cross and the bronze serpent have become symbols that God wants sin and suffering to end, that we can exchange these symbols of torture for images of healing and redemption. Having repudiated the fear and oppression, the cross and the serpent can represent tools for renewal and healing. Moreover, we are also free to choose new symbols of comfort, growth, and life. Suffering and healing are journey, process, risk, and hope. So far I have learned that we struggle, lift our eyes, and move on.

Yes I Can!
Gail Christy *Speaks*

I was born over 50 years ago and from the very beginning I was an impatient child. I was expected March 21 but arrived at tea time (4:30 p.m.) January 13—10 1/2 weeks early! I was not expected to survive but with God's grace and my own determination, which I am sure operated from day one, I lived.

My early arrival had consequences and at the age of two, when I was still not walking, but talking in sentences, I was diagnosed as having cerebral palsy. Cerebral palsy is a static condition of motor impairment caused by damage to the motor area of the brain before, during, or after birth. This diagnosis began my long association with the medical system. It is a system that has, for the most part, served me well. I met, in my many hospital stays, many nurses and doctors whom I am sure were heaven sent. But I recognize that I was listened to, in this system, because I was both clever and articulate. And I wasn't part of it for very long. After three surgeries, the medical people largely ignored me. I guess it was because there was not hope of curing me. My brain was the culprit.

Cerebral palsy is not glamorous. You can look funny, talk funny, and have terrible difficulty with movement and there is the added reality that one may also have developmental or intellectual difficulties. Even if you do not, people make haste to ascribe them to you because of the way you look or the way you act.

To be honest, I have often wished I could lie and say I had had polio. Polio somehow has always seemed to me to be a more acceptable disability. Perhaps it was because polio was an illness that could strike randomly. It randomly struck important people, for example, Franklin D. Roosevelt, and so there was a lot of attention paid to it. Research was done.

In the beginning, I was a happy kid going to a special school. I do not think this happiness that I felt was because of my family. They were not all that sympathetic and certainly did not understand what it was like, either to be a child or a child with a disability. I remember my mother accusing me of being "so jealous" of my younger brother. I remember I used to feel very puzzled at that comment. Why would I not have felt anger at my brother? He could run and play while I could do neither and the neighbourhood kids made fun of me!

I remember that when I had my operations and was in a body cast for months at a time, my brother was not happy with all the attention that I got. I have always thought that surgery was a high price to pay for attention.

While I might have felt estranged from my family, I always had a sense that God understood and was holding me in care.

Even though I had braces and went to a special school, I did not regard myself as different from other youngsters. However, I soon realized that I was different in one respect; at about age seven, I had settled on a vocational goal. I knew that I wanted to be a teacher of grade two or six. I observed my teachers closely and, when I was 11, I began to collect resources for this career.

The time came to enter teachers' college and I applied with joyful anticipation. My admission form told them that I had cerebral palsy. Back came a swift reply from the admissions people. It was not acceptance but a request to see them immediately in view of what I had told them about having cerebral palsy. I also had to see the doctor who examined prospective students for teachers' college. He was a heart specialist. I do not recall now much about the interview but I remember being puzzled by the question, "Can you write?" They were referring, not to my creativity, but rather to the mechanics of writing. I replied that " Yes, I wrote as badly as everybody else." Some said I was too smart-alecky.

Despite a plea to the Minister of Education, I was refused admission because of my "insupportable" disability.

It was suggested that I train as a speech pathologist.

I took the first step and obtained my B.A. from Carleton University in 1965. The activities around my request to enter Speech Pathology and Audiology training at the University of Toronto echoed my earlier difficulties. Initially I was refused but my family brought political pressure to bear and at the last minute I was admitted. I remember having difficulty finding a place to live because people did not want the responsibility of having someone with a disability in their home.

My time at the University of Toronto was absolutely horrendous, although I will always treasure the friends I made in my co-op house. But in the speech pathology department, I was harassed and lied about from the very beginning. I think the hope was that I would leave voluntarily. I did not. I completed the course but was not graduated. I never believed that I was that unintelligent. I had cerebral palsy because of damage to the motor area of my brain but my intellect was always intact.

It was hard enough to be faced with a transcript that read "failure" but what I also almost lost was my spirit. I can still feel, if I think about it, the abandonment I felt: absolutely alone and with no one, friends or family, to understand. God had certainly departed. Friends were sympathetic but at the same time I felt that they just did not have the resources to devote to this injustice.

After Toronto, I returned to Ottawa and was hired by the Ottawa Board of Education as its first speech pathologist. I worked in the same school I had attended as a youngster. Later, I worked as a counsellor, worked part-time on a degree in counselling, and then met the man I married, Robert Christy. Bob and I had met originally at a hospital speech clinic where I was the interested student and he was the patient coming for stuttering therapy.

For several years, life was pleasant and calm, or relatively so when you have two youngsters. Then I felt called to ministry. We all had an exciting and busy three years as Mom got educated.

Off to Yellow Grass we all flew. It was a good three years as the Christys and the pastoral charge learned from each other. I have often marvelled at the faith of that pastoral charge. They knew I did not drive and they knew that I was disabled yet they said, "Yes" to us. Initially, my ordination was in doubt because a settlement church could not be found. Not much was said but I know my disability was an issue. The settlement person from my home Conference did make a contribution. He called just before final exams to say I could not be settled and offered to give me the phone number of a friend of his who had hand controls on his car. I did not take the number.

After three years in Yellow Grass, I was called to Carmichael United Church in Regina to follow a man who was retiring after 17 years. It was not a happy time.

Many factors contributed to this unhappiness. But it was also clear that many of the elderly congregation could not look beyond the difficulty I have in walking. For example, when my name was recommended to the congregation, one of the questions asked was, "How will she do her housework?" I was not being hired as the church janitor. I will always remember a pastoral visit I made to a "dissatisfied" couple. Two things will remain with me: the hate in the voice of the woman as she said, "I was just devastated on August 3, 1986 [my first Sunday] when I saw you in the pulpit!" I also recall my own surprise at the realization that, although this woman had always attended church ("I remember going with mother in the horse and buggy," she said), it was quite clear that the gospel message of love and acceptance had not penetrated. I can smile now when I think of her husband, trying in the name of courtesy(?) to keep his wife from saying what was really on her mind, "Now, Honey, that's enough."

In that dark time, I again felt abandoned by God and was sorely tempted to leave ministry. However, if I had done that, then the Church would have been freed from having to deal with discrimination in its midst. It is harder to ignore injustice when you see it in front of you. But I also realized that again, I was very much supported by friends and former parishioners. The care and concern that came my way, at that dark time in Regina, touched me profoundly. The memories of that support are a resource that I draw upon. Those memories of support still nourish my soul.

The Psalms have always been a source of strength and comfort to me. I love the full range of emotions that are to be found there. They are a resource for any event of daily life. When I was a beginning theological student, I gave myself a "project" and turned all the Psalms into prayers or other worship resources. When the invitation came to participate in this project, I returned yet again to the Psalms and sought to look at them using the lenses of a woman living with a disability. I offer some commentary on two favourite Psalms:

Psalm 23

The Divine Shepherd

The Lord is my shepherd, I shall not want.
You make me lie down in green pastures;
You lead me beside still waters;
You restore my soul.
You lead me in the paths of righteousness
for Your name's sake.
Even though I walk through the darkest valley,
I fear no evil; for You are with me;
Your rod and Your staff—they comfort me.
You prepare a table before me
in the presence of my enemies;
You anoint my head with oil;
My cup overflows.

> *Surely goodness and mercy shall follow me*
> * all the days of my life,*
> *And I shall dwell in Your house*
> * my whole life long.*

For me, this is a psalm of great comfort. I know that only the presence of God has enabled me to walk through, however clumsily, the dark valleys of my life. At times, it seemed that I was going to be forever stuck in these valleys, but I have endured and been able to walk through to the other side. My own cane (staff) has been a great help.

I am grateful, God, because You have shown my enemies (society) that I can serve You, the Lord. I am able to be of service. My only prayer is to continue to serve in Your temple.

Psalm 62:5–8a
Song of Trust in God Alone

> *For God alone my soul waits in silence,*
> * for my hope is from God.*
> *God alone is my rock and my salvation,*
> * my fortress; I shall not be shaken.*
> *On God rests my deliverance and my honour;*
> * my mighty rock, my refuge is in God.*
> *Trust in God at all times.*

I struggle to have the words of this psalm serve as my creed. My refuge is God and I know that no matter what my state of mind, God will understand and allow me to speak from my heart. I trust God to understand.

These verses sum up my attitude to God as I greet each new day.

Someone asked me recently if there was any joy in living with a disability. I think there is, mostly because of the people I encounter. I consider that I have been most blessed by so many of the people who have entered my life.

In addition, living with a disability has challenged me to think and reflect deeply about God's world and my place in it, the place of all those, in fact, who do not meet the "norm." I think that I have been allowed to live life more deeply than most and I am grateful. I truly rejoice that I have been able to use the God-given gifts I have in this time and this place in God's world.

A Vision of Justice

One of the things I think about, in the time I set aside to envisage a different kind of world, is a society where there will be justice for all people who live with disability or chronic illness. No one would be excluded. When I think of justice, several areas come to mind, all important for people with disabilities, and I would like to deal with each in turn. When services for people with disabilities are being evaluated, these are the five areas that are considered: access, transportation, education, employment, and recreation. I would also like to look at language (and law). Physical access to a facility is probably the most important item to be considered because, without access, no amount of special services will be helpful.

I would hope that in a society where there is justice, access would simply be a non-issue. There would be no entrance stairs, no heavy doors, and all parts of a building would be equally accessible; no longer would there be arguments about the cost of re-designing inaccessible buildings because those buildings would be accessible from drawing-board conception to completion. No longer would getting around in society be an endurance test; no longer would society be able to practise the oppression that physical barriers represent.[50] No longer would we have some of the senseless mistakes of the past like a rehabilitation centre approached by a long, lovely ramp with a huge step at the bottom of it! No longer would places of worship be continually out of reach for people living with disabilities. No longer would the act of worship be a source of frustration, exclusion, and pain.

But access is not just a question of ramps and automatic doors, proper lighting and closed captions, or signing interpretation at a poetry reading. It is a question of attitude. In our present society, there is a problem with access because, somehow, there is the message that some people are more valuable or worthy than others, that disability equals incompetence and inferiority.[51] Is this the reason why, even in churches that are accessible, the pulpit is usually not? In a just society, we would automatically seek inclusion because we would know that no one is excluded. We all depend on one another. No one is inferior and there is no condescension. I have to say that I have often encountered people and institutions who look down their noses at me. I guess because I do not expect it, I remember with most pain the rehabilitation centres and churches where I bumped up against discrimination. The rehabilitation centres would call to give me appointments for the doctor (God) and could not understand that I had other claims on my time. The assumption was that I had nothing to do except attend rehabilitation appointments.

In the church, the condescension came out in the form of not so subtle questions: are you really a delegate to presbytery? Or to another companion: is she really a minister? Or in the case of my husband: a total non-response to his request for confirmation.

Transportation tailored to the needs of disabled people is today a reality for many and believe me, I often thank God for it. However, I wonder if a just society would be a society where there was no distinction, no separation of disabled people and able-bodied people. I have observed that separate transportation systems sets up a "them" and "us" mentality. As well, the spectre of jealousy raises it head. There are those people who resent the door-to-door aspect of special transportation.

Equal access to education and equal quality of education is something that is crucial in a just society. I had a good time and was a good student during my elementary and high school years. When I was refused access to higher education, it came as a heart-stopping shock. Today there is greater access but there are handicapping attitudes within the system. Teachers may not want "exceptional" students in their classes so students may well and truly be in a situation that is incorrect for them. Yet people lack the courage to make the necessary changes.

In a just society, there would be no need for employment equity.

In a just society, recreational pursuits of many kinds would be equally available to all. My needs in this area have always been met but when I think about it, I have noticed a preponderance of swimming activities and a dearth of cultural events. For example, I have only seen signing at one poetry reading. The cost of a ticket for a symphony concert is beyond the reach of many people living with disabilities or they can not see as well as they would like because they have to sit at the back of the concert hall to comply with fire regulations.

I can not leave this look at a just society without a look at language. Language and attitude go hand in hand.

When I was a child, the term used in education circles for students like myself was "exceptional." I never heard that term in a negative way. I thought we were exceptional kids. We rode a neat bus to school; the drivers were good; so were the teachers. We had parties, we learned things, we laughed a lot, and always had lots of visitors at the school.

We also did a lot of lovely handwork at school and for a long time I thought that handwork (which I did well, except for sewing) and handicap were the same word. When I discovered this was not so, I refused, and still refuse, to use the word "handicap." It is very clear to me that my life is a statement that I am not handicapped.

However, I grudgingly acknowledge that I am "technically" disabled because my body is not as "able" as some others. I do need things, like a cane and railings, but I will not be defined solely by that need.

I dislike the words "physically challenged" because attention is directed away from the cause of these challenges. I am, it is true, physically challenged but that has nothing to do with my action, but rather is due to the barriers that present society erects. Nor am I a "victim of" or "afflicted with" cerebral palsy. I happen to have a medical condition called cerebral palsy.

I believe that the fact that I have cerebral palsy is a random event, connected with the fact that I am human, but not connected, in any way, to a wish on the part of God to punish my parents or to punish me. What on earth can an infant do to offend God? Yet that belief, that people with disabilities are afflicted [sic] that way because they are bad and God is punishing them, is still common. I heard myself described that way 30 years ago and today, we hear AIDS described (and dismissed) as God's punishment.

I believe there is a way to a just society. We need to be taught how to carry out the translation into action. My vision is that someday we will be able to do that.

Questioning Everything
Barb Elliott *Speaks*

A tribute to Barb Elliott was written by Brian Brennan in the Calgary Herald *at her death in November, 1992. Brennan says, "For most of her life, Barb Elliott suffered from a chronic lung disorder. During her last six years, she had to carry oxygen with her everywhere. But she didn't define herself by her disability. She defined herself as a woman, as a feminist, and as a Christian who passionately believed in social justice." This chapter is compiled and edited by Charlotte Caron from things that Barb wrote or said on tape over the last 15 to 20 years of her life and reflects the truth of Brennan's words.*

I arrived at middle age with a whole new passion about working with women, about theology, about justice issues and their interconnections. It has been so exciting. I would not trade these last 10 to 15 years. I am moved by the strength and beauty I see among women. I am wistful that we still have many things to learn about supporting each other. I am hopeful that women in community will continue to make their collective voice strongly heard and their presence effective for justice-making in the world.

As we began, here in Saskatchewan, to explore Christian feminism, we became both energized and overwhelmed by the seemingly endless implications. We could see how the Christian tradition supported patriarchy. Were there revolutionary seeds in the tradition, as well, with which we could identify as we examined our experience as women, and as we began the push for change? At the 1980 annual meeting of Conference we introduced a motion for the use of inclusive language in the Saskatchewan United Church. What about female imagery for God? Women lined up at the mikes and it was an unexpectedly moving experience. Somewhat to our surprise, the motion passed. However, a storm of hostile reaction followed in the next months, and still occasionally takes its toll in energy.

Is it possible to stay within the present church and take seriously the feminist agenda to which we have become committed? Many of us live on the edges, nurturing and encouraging one another, never far from the questions and doubts, yet knowing the tradition has done much to mould us.

As we reached out around us, both in the cities and the rural areas, we found response from many women. Together we have read and studied; we have organized gatherings. We have shared stories, information, and support. We have attempted to organize a network to operate without hierarchy. We have struggles with not wanting to be tied to church structures, particularly in relation to budget and accountability. Sometimes, however, we do want access to dialogue and challenge. We also value The United Church of Canada's involvement on issues such as pornography and its pro-choice position on abortion. At other times we want to call the church to account for its destructiveness to women.

We have found it is not easy to "exorcise the internalized patriarchal presence"[52] in each of us. This is partly because we are not clear what to put in its place. We must be willing to build towards an unknown, step by step, and be willing to risk newness. I personally find it exhausting, but necessary, especially working in a patriarchal institution like the church, to ask myself about everything that I think or do, "Is this consistent with a feminist perspective?" It colours everything that I am. And I have never learned to compromise.

Early in the life of our network I realized that articles were an excellent means of enabling busy women to be in touch with what feminist writers, including theologians, were thinking. After consultation, we decided to do regular mailings of articles to any women interested. Thus was born *The Unbeaten Path,* which is still being published three times a year, and goes to over 100 women, now on a subscription basis.[53] We try to choose some radical articles to push us all. Two wonderful women have co-edited with me. Readers contribute. The response is enthusiastic, especially from farm women who may not have another like-minded woman close by to talk to.

This publication mainly goes to committed feminists, but also works as a consciousness-raiser. It is exciting to hear a woman who, a few years ago, was saying some very traditional things, coming out with a radical statement of analysis. I think to myself, "Does she hear herself? Does she realize how far she has travelled? Does she know how it may change her life?" Such moments make me catch my breath and also give me encouragement for the long haul.

We always include a section in *The Unbeaten Path* on global feminism. I need to hear experiences and opinions out of different contexts with an open mind to allow for a different framework and meaning.

And what wonderfully intelligent, strong, and caring women live in all parts of the globe! It is so energizing to read their words, to hear about what women are doing, and have been doing for a long time. There is much despair, of course, for the times when it seems like enormous amounts of organizing and energy have gone for nothing or very little, or have even made things worse. But there seems to be a persistence here which gives hope. I am surer than ever that the women's movement is very much alive and moving.

A fairly common thread is the ambiguity that all traditional religions seem to hold for women. Over and over it sounds clear that religious roots are really important, that religion is both a source of ideals and a source of energy and vision for women. Yet it is equally clear that religious ideals and religious communities are places where women have been marginalized and drastically oppressed. Another voice I am beginning to hear repeatedly is that fundamentalism is on the upsurge in many places and is a real worry to women.

I have never really been emotionally invested in "ecumenical work," such as interfaith dialogue, but when it comes to being in relation with women of other countries and traditions, in mutual support and solidarity, around urgent needs for social change, around life and death issues, that's a whole different thing. Does it really matter what religious or cultural label goes on our feminism? Maybe feminist theology/spirituality is the framework that can move us together to a new place, bringing together the best of the old traditions plus new reflections on experience, shared experience.

The sad thing is how we all, women included, have, in Mary Daly's words, "an internalized patriarchal presence." We are sometimes able to "exorcise" this; but too often we women give our power away. Even when we see the reality of what is happening, we are torn. The price is high. If we name it, or resist it, we run the risk of disapproval or rejection by those in power, and even the risk of physical danger to ourselves.

We are not popular if we call people to account on things. This is especially so in the area of disability. I see what no one else is doing and start doing it. But I do not know if I am doing much. I am trying to deal with disabilities and health things but I am not very successful. I feel like people just think it is me wanting stuff for myself. Both society and the church are nowhere in terms of dealing with disabilities.

I have had a breathing disability called bronchiectasis for most of my life. It moved into being a visible disability when I went on oxygen about five years ago. I found I had to start dealing more with how people react to me because I felt that people looked at me now that I carry a tank of liquid oxygen with me. People in our society, in patriarchy if you like, notice anything that is not the norm, whatever the norm is. I have good friends in Berkeley who helped me with this. One in particular, Betsy, who uses a wheelchair said to me, "At first I hated the wheelchair, but," she said, "it wasn't very long in fact before I didn't pay any attention to people looking at me. I didn't even notice that they were. I couldn't care less." That is exactly what I found with carrying the oxygen. Soon I forgot about it. I didn't pay any attention to people looking at me and couldn't care less. In fact, sometimes when I see someone looking at me, I wonder what they are looking at. I have almost forgotten myself sometimes.

I have had to move to half-time employment. Some folks think this means I have lots of spare time. They do not understand that for me to work half-time is the same as for most people to work full-time. I spend at least one hour a day on nebulizing, one hour on postural drainage, and it takes me longer to get dressed, wash my hair, and all of the tasks of daily living. In addition, I estimate that it takes on average one and one-half hours a day to go to doctor's appointments, do the paperwork for medical claims, phone the oxygen company, go to Saskatchewan Aids to Independent Living, wash equipment, and the other health related things I need to do. There are not enough hours in the day to be working more than half time.

Another friend in Berkeley, Jean, has lupus. We have talked a lot about the embarrassment we feel when people ask us how we are. We continually want to be able to reassure them and say we are fine. In reality, we are not. In our society, you should either be well or dead. It's an either/or proposition. For the average person that may fit. But there's the rub. The average person. I bother others because I am not going to get well. I think for many of us the idea of a continuum would be better. On a scale of 1 to 10, where are you today? Or some other kinds of categories that would indicate that that is where our lives are lived, neither sick nor well, but struggling somewhere in there. When I describe how I am feeling on any given day, I am not complaining, not pleading for sympathy, and not expecting you to fix things. I am saying that these are my parameters today and it is given as information for our relating.

I have begun to explore questions about the relation of independence, interdependence, and dependence. I have always been independent. But now I wonder how much longer I can go on living this way. How do we find mutuality when one woman's needs change and she becomes increasingly dependent? My condition is not the same from day to day. Sometimes I need certain things done and sometimes I do not want it done for me by someone else. How can I maintain the independence I need and yet have help with things when I need it?

This leads me to thinking about having control of our bodies. I want a cause and effect. I am sure we all do, so therefore if I get a little worse, I struggle to figure out why. What did I do, what did I not do? What would explain this in order that it won't happen again? I hear that idea from other people too. "Oh," they will say to me, "Did you get overtired? Did you get a new virus?" Sometimes the questions make me feel like I must be responsible. It is as if something I did or did not do put me on the downhill again. There seems to be a fear of bodies, that everyone is supposed to have control of their body. But the cause and effect approach does not work. One summer I learned a big lesson. I went off for two weeks of holidays. I had a wonderful time, and came back feeling rested, relaxed, really healthy. I went to bed and woke up about three in the morning bleeding from my lungs. What I realized was, I don't have control over what happens. That was the first time I really acknowledged that I don't have control. That is pretty scary.

But people need as much control as possible. We need to be able to recognize that we are still agents in the world. Often because you don't have control over your health, you need it over some part of your life. I often become distressed if plans get changed, if people change the times or days when things are going to happen. I also know that sometimes I have to change plans because of my health. So I need a combination of planning ahead but with contingency plans. Cheri Register writes about the difficulty of making plans that she may not be able to keep, and yet being discontented with living with "no plans beyond bedtime." I struggle with the same dilemmas she raises: how to make a difference in our imperfect world, how to make commitments without wondering 'what if I get sick and cannot do this?' and how to make long term plans wondering if I will be able to see them through. Like her, "I want to know the agenda. I want to solve the problems before they arise ... "[54]

Another area of struggling is over how strong we are supposed to be. People will tell me about other people they know that have this or that wrong with them and they are always so brave and they are always so cheerful about it. Sometimes I feel like saying, "I have no intention of being cheerful! Or strong." We do what we do because we really do not have much alternative.

Yet there is an expectation of no complaints from us. It seems that the choices are being strong or being blamed.

Another thing I think is that people feel that they miss or they grieve for the old Barb, the one that could work all night if she had to, and do one workshop after another, and had lots of energy. Some relationships feel unresolved. And yes, I am different than I used to be. But what I would like to say to people is that I've learned a lot. People think that it is all loss, but there have been gains for me in this disability. I see many things differently, see from a different perspective, through a different lens. People, situations, life, and death are re-focused from here. I've learned a lot. But because people see me as "less than" now, they do not seem to want my learning. Now that's generalizing, but I have that sense.

In carrying this oxygen, or by having this chronic condition, I have started to get a lot more clear about the difference between the charity and the justice model in treating people who are not the group in power. I have been able to apply that back to feminism and to come to much more clarity there too. Charity (which is often out of the liberal point of view) requires gratefulness. We are to be grateful, rather than simply having a basic human right that can allow us to have dignity. Charity is people thinking they know what I need and doing it for me without asking me if it is, in fact, what I do need—as when someone gets me a sweater because I am coughing and they assume I am cold. Or buys cheap tissues (which I cannot use) or a huge box of laundry soap (that I cannot lift) because they want to save me money. Justice is people treating me with dignity, listening to what I need and providing it because I need it, not because they need to do it for me or out of pity.

Liberalism blocks liberation. Most of us have liberalism in our bones. By liberalism I am referring to that ideology which took root during the Enlightenment culture in the eighteenth and nineteenth centuries. Liberalism trusts individual judgement and reason over received authority. It believes in the power of education and reform to create change. All people are to be considered equal, and there is a belief in progress. Liberalism also sees society as pluralistic, with a variety of beliefs and viewpoints to be tolerated and accepted and kept in balance.

Liberal theology meant faithfulness was seen as the individual responsibility before God. There has been a real tolerance of pluralism and different points of view. The openness of liberalism has been a big factor in allowing discussion to happen in recent years about sexism and heterosexism, both in church and in society. Much of the support for feminists comes out of the liberal stream. Much of liberalism sounds great to be a part of.

A shadow side is the liberal emphasis on individualism. Feminism values the individual. But if we focus exclusively on this, we undermine the possibility of community. If we concentrate only on women's individual growth and well-being and sense of freedom, let's not kid ourselves that anything will necessarily be changed at all in society. What would it mean to put community in the centre? We need to develop a sense of accountability: to continually ask ourselves, To whom am I/are we accountable? The only possibility for changing society lies in working together in community.

Liberalism says you have to be "fair" to everybody. But liberation theology talks about a preferential option for the poor.

God is for and with the oppressed. Do we believe this? Do we take it seriously? If so, then our attention must be on those people who are poor, those who are oppressed, women, people of colour, people with disabilities, and so on. It is rather like affirmative action. And we are not distracted by, "But what about the rich?" (or "What about the men?") The question becomes, "Who are my people?" in any given situation. And having identified "my people," to ask whether they stand to gain or to lose.

As liberalism stresses fairness, liberation thinking stresses justice—for the oppressed. Do we let ourselves get hooked too much on being fair? Liberalism often talks about equality as "sameness," without much thought about whether we all start in the same place, or whether there is a power differential. So let's not be too quick to say, "That seems fair." The question is not whether we are treating everyone the same, but rather whether we are moving towards equity, more equal opportunity. The question is, "Is this just?" Does this give justice to the oppressed? People with disabilities may need access in order to have an equal starting place.

The challenge is to be more aware when liberalism is actually stopping us in our tracks, often with pleasant smiles and "reasonable arguments." We need good questions to help us challenge assumptions, and discern the more radical or liberation way to go if there is to be justice for all women.

Justice is people being able to have some freedom to experience their lives yet know what kind of restrictions to place on themselves so others can have that freedom too. I read a lot of feminist Utopian literature. I think that justice means opportunity for everyone to experience something positive in their lives. There are masses of people in other countries who are starving. Survival is their only goal and even that is not possible for very long. How would they know that it is okay to be alive?

Justice is meeting the basic needs of food and shelter. It means some people giving up some of what they have and that is what is difficult. We need to learn that this does not mean the same thing for everyone. What is essential is for everyone to have equal access to the necessary resources for their lives and for each life to be respected.

My increasing disability means that I always understand the difference between justice and charity in new ways. I get insights that go beyond the disability. Charity too much involves the un-mutual interchange that is patronizing and demeaning of the person. Justice means that it does not matter if you like the person, that they are entitled to your respect and are given some access to responsibilities. Much of our attitude towards the disabled has been charity. But I refuse to spend my life being grateful!

Equal access does not mean treating everyone the same but in allowing everyone access to the resources that they need to live. Affirmative action is based in that and so is seen by many as unfair. They cannot see that to be equal some people need to be given accessibility.

Community and support are what make justice. Community and support create a sense of belonging to something greater than ourselves—world wide, infinite, eternal.

Back in 1972 I wrote that what is important in life is being able to love, being able to accept love, being involved in giving and receiving support from others, being able to risk, to be extravagant. It is liking yourself even when you goof, and having enough confidence and competence to be able to do some of the things you want and need to do and which seem worthwhile to the world's life. It is having some friends along the way who are honest and real and care, with whom to share.

In 1985, I was offered a Doctor of Divinity by St. Andrew's College. I declined because I do not want this kind of recognition. This kind of individual recognition does not seem consistent with the things I have believed in or have been working for in the church. As I have worked with laity, and in recent years particularly with women, I have become more and more convinced that we must change the system to eliminate oppression. I want to emphasize community, mutuality, equality in the church; and I reject the parts of the system which seem to me to foster status, separation, or any kind of hierarchy.

I still believe that community is central. It is crucial to feel part of a community somewhere (family, church, a group, etc.). Those of us with disabilities wonder who is going to hang in with us. For me, the physiotherapists at the Regina General Hospital provide my strongest sense of community. They have past experience of losing people but they have not let that stop them from significant relationships with me as I go for treatment every day. It must cost them to create community with their patients. But they do it. I find that there is power in being together with the physiotherapists and with other communities of which I am a part. We are strengthened by each other.

In *God's Fierce Whimsy*, Bev Harrison uses the image of God as an electric current, a kind of connector.[55] I think the Spirit works in relation, between people. So it is theological to do things together. I do believe that there is more energy in it if it comes out of the group. I have a deep belief that when two people are together, more than one plus one happens. It is not that I can not do it myself but I am so much more alive if there is more than one planning and presenting. There is some kind of aliveness; spirit happens when people come together. Community, love, justice, nurturing that is life-giving: these are important. There is also something—some wisdom, love, power that is beyond rational thought—beyond what one can explain.

I was starting to image some kind of femaleness around God and unless that is true I do not have any connection with ultimate reality in the universe. Whatever it is—spirit, something that happens between people—has to be as much female as male or I will not have anything to do with it. So I made it very female. It is really hard not to do some embodiment imaging like Nelle Morton talking about imaging Her next to her on the plane.[56]

Somewhere in there most of my theology and understanding of church got reframed. Everything I did/do had to stand the test: "Is this consistent with a feminist perspective?" Always asking that question is very exhausting. I was always asking, "What is going on here?" I drove everyone crazy including myself.

I am in a different space now. Being through a family crisis with
Mom having a stroke and my brother, Alan, having a heart attack
within two weeks of each other, and then, when Mom died, I have
had to think about a lot of things. I have nothing to put in the
place of the theology that does not fit any more. There is a
loneliness and a scariness about that. It probably has been that
way for a long time but I had not identified that so much of it was
not meaningful. To totally disconnect feels like ripping out a part of
my roots. Yet a lot of what is going on in Christianity is
destructive. A lot of women's predicament is perpetuated by
Christian tradition. But where did I get the ideas of love and
justice if not through Christian tradition? Goddess worship just
does not do it for me. I can not create a religion on my own.

I have been studying global feminism for the last several years.
Women globally are much more traditional in Christianity than are
North American women. They live in such a different context
than we do. The culture in Asia is not Christian. I want to have
much more of a world in which we are learning to live together—
to be together in the world and in community. Whatever religion
promotes life-giving, caring justice has to be okay. We do not have
to agree with the specific components if this is what it does. If it is
destructive, it is useless. Every major religion has been both. Did I
grow up with a sense of justice because of or in spite of
Christianity? or family? or experiences? I don't know that. Is there
anything beyond humanism or working for justice? Does there
need to be more?

We need good questions to help us challenge assumptions, and
discern the more radical and liberating way to go. We need to
question everything! What are the alternatives? Who would
benefit from this? What will this mean for women? Which
women? Where would power be? Would this be oppressive to
any group? What are the implications? What are the other
options? What would it mean if we could be in solidarity with
women around the globe working to transform radically the
structures in which we live our lives?

There are profound theological questions raised by living with a disability. There are issues of self-esteem: Am I okay? What is the meaning of my life here? How do we maintain self respect? Are we more than our value as producers? Do I have intrinsic value as being in God's image? How do I want to spend these last days? Can I live with integrity as if I have an open-ended future? Do we as disabled women benefit society? Does our society have responsibility so we can be productive? Should it not be possible for everyone to have what they need to be out and about? We are constantly caught up in doing the accommodating to other people; when is it the community's responsibility to accommodate? How can we understand each other's embodiment? How can we live maximally in an ongoing way especially as disability increases? What can help us as we re-assess our values? What helps us learn and grow? Who is going to hang in with me for the long haul? Who has responsibility for bearing the cost?

I struggle with the meaning of life. Is it okay for me to be alive? I need to know that. Has my life been of any significance or have I wasted it? Am I worried about the dying process? What do I need to build into my life around that? We've already lost so much— our health, etc. What is left to lose? If I do not spend time worrying about dying, I must at core level believe that love and caring are in ultimate charge in the world. But what about all the questions about self agency regarding death, about the technology to keep one alive and about quality of life and who pulls the plug?

In terms of health care I see where things fit in. I am trying to deal with disabilities and health care as my way of working for justice in the world. I push for access and I have what I need but most of the world does not so it makes me feel kind of funny. I was struck by a quote by Bonnie Klein when she said, "Non-disabled people are an obstacle in my world."[57] There is such a tide of prejudice against disabilities these days! But we all have to do what we can. What I ask is that you take me seriously. Being able to be who I am is vital—to be authentic—for there is nowhere else to start. We have to disentangle the interconnections of the personal and systemic so that sound analysis will lead to clear strategy. Present the problem, vision the possibility, seek the promise, accept our power.

I am where I am. I do not feel finished. I need to be exposed, challenged and renewed. I need something to help me be nurtured. And yet I enjoy the glorious absurdities of being human! I've learned a lot.

Conversations
Hearing Each Other into Speech

In *The Journey Is Home* Nelle Morton writes about "hearing each other into speech."[58] As a Collective, part of our process was conversation. Talking/listening allowed us to dig more deeply into our lives and our experiences, to say things that we had not said before. We heard each other into speech. We share part of some conversations with you. Not all of the members of the Collective were present for all of the conversations so some voices are not as frequent as others who were able to be part of the whole event. As well some women participated as recorders of the conversations.

Joan: Friendship as a political act jumps out as impor-
          tant. It seems right.

Liz: In our society, we tend to be objectified when we
          are identified as persons with disabilities. Objects
          don't make friends; human people living make
          friends. That's political. We are part of society. As
          part of society, when I befriend, I take myself
          seriously and take the other seriously. It may be in

moments of friendship, those moments when there is an "I–Thou" relationship or in a long enduring relationship. Friendship is based upon the dignity of human care and interaction.

Sharon: Disability moves into the political only when we become necessary—only in so far as we can be used to get a vote.

Liz: Or make somebody some dollars! We are only served as it becomes economically viable.

Joan: That is depressing to think about. Is everything connected to the almighty dollar?

Elinor: I heard an interview on the radio recently with John McKnight, a community development innovator. He was talking about people living with a variety of disabilities. He asked, "How many people are in this person's life who are not paid to be there?" It is a political statement when we, or our society, opt out of friendships because people or agencies or institutions can be paid to be in our lives. The question hit me because sometimes it has seemed to me that my lifeline has been people who are paid.

Liz: Barb reversed that. It was the physiotherapists who were paid to be there who were very important to her.

Elinor: But I have also felt pathologized. I found people did not want to be around me and people who had been my friends were no longer close. I had to be resourceful enough to pay people for support.

Christine: But it is not actually paying people to be your friends. It comes about.

Elinor: Some caregivers do become friends. When I had a very small circle of friends I needed the paid caregivers. Part of my goal has been to expand my circle, and gradually I have.

Joan: I think about my relationship with the nurse who helped me with my diabetes. I had her home number and her work number. When I first was diabetic, I did not know what I was supposed to be like. So I could phone her and say this is what is happening. The doctor had said this is what is supposed to happen, but I did not respond in the way the books said I would. I remember thinking at the time, "Gee, I can't even get being sick right!" My nurse would say, "We'll figure it out." There was information in books but I wasn't typical. She would advocate with the endocrinologist. She taught me I had the answers and I needed help to find the answer.

             When I moved to Fort McMurray, I really missed her. I was saying that to someone and she said, "Why don't you call her?" I realized I phone my friends, so I could phone her. She had become my friend.

Elinor: I celebrate resources! But it depends on us having economic resources and on the risks we are willing to take to have access to those. Some were not available to my mother's and grandmother's generations and still may not be available depending on economics or geographic location.

Jayne: I think of the book by Carter Heyward, *When Boundaries Betray Us.*[59] That book raises questions about being paid and being friends, and about differences in power relationships. We have to constantly monitor boundaries, especially when therapists become friends or friends become therapists. We need to ensure there is balance in both aspects of the relationship. If we identify ourselves as disabled, people are willing to leap in and fix us. That means we have to monitor boundaries in relationships and seek balance between the friendship part and the therapist part of the relationship.

Sharon: There is a difference in people who are paid. I would not want to say that people who are paid do not care; they do. I have a different relationship with those people who are paid, whether or not it is an ongoing relationship, than with someone who lives in my home or who comes in. For example, sometimes people come into our homes—people who are our friends and do the things that we need to have done. They accept that we do not need those things done all of the time, but sometimes we do.

Gail: Because one is disabled, people can assume you do not know what is going on. With medical people you are a CP on the examining table, not a person. You have to educate them even though society says you should not teach educated people. Once my orthopaedic surgeon was doing a video on me. There was a new kind of surgery, so I was taken around and shown off as his specimen, his work. Once one of the other surgeons asked when I had had my surgery. The doctor gave the wrong date and I corrected him. My mother said, "Oh Gail, Dr. A. would know." I was 13 at the time so I did not say, "Excuse me BUT ..." I knew but was not given credit for knowing about my life. The doctor was God, was always right.

Christine: Physiotherapists seem to realize that bodies are different. There is such a variety in cerebral palsy. They do not have standard sessions for all of us. They are always dealing with different things.

Sharon: When someone is dealing with multiple disabilities with a specialist who deals with only one thing, there is no recognition of other parts of my body. They say, "Do this" but I can't because of some other disability. It feels to me like no one in the medical profession has a holistic approach.

Liz: We are also vulnerable to other's perceptions of boundaries. I can get over-fatigued quite easily. Sometimes I unexpectedly need help to get from point A to point B and do not have a cane with me. One day when this happened I asked someone I knew quite well if I could take his arm. He let me take his arm but said "I better not let my wife see this." Perceiving a sexual boundary at that time was not appropriate. Help with walking was what I needed.

People also think that just because my body does not function that they can invade my personal space. When I am using a wheelchair, people will touch or push me in ways which I do not want and that they would never do to other "able-bodied" people. Their perception of usual cultural boundaries becomes altered or distorted.

Gail: Was it in humour that this man commented about his wife?

Liz: No, I think it was in fear. Some people are so afraid of disability that I will not ask them for help; I would sit on the street for an hour before I would ask them to touch me. Some people are so uncomfortable with their own bodies that they are repulsed when mine is out of control. They find it difficult to become physically close to me so make attempts at explanations or humour, or they have to leave the scene.

But humour is a strange thing. It can cover up so many feelings.

Sharon: Some of the remarks that people think are funny are really insulting and rude.

Joan: Hurtful!

Liz: Demeaning.

Christine: Everybody is afraid of becoming disabled in a car accident, or from diving into a shallow pool, of what could happen.

Joan: And so they are afraid of us.

Elinor: In *A Leg to Stand On,* Oliver Sacks writes about this from the perspective of a neurophysiologist.[60] Sacks severed a tendon while mountain climbing. As a doctor, he became a patient and he writes about the profound dislocation from himself that he experienced because of his injury. He has a wonderful chapter on convalescence—that time between the crisis time and the time of being independent. He noted a strong "us-them" mentality between the staff and "patients" in the convalescent facility.

As angry as I feel about it, I think this is a very human instinct. It must somehow be linked to survival! It must be a strategy. I don't think it is just being unkind.

Joan: One of my friends says, "I never know how to respond around people with disabilities."

Christine: I was talking to a friend about people with disabilities. The friend said, "I don't know what to say. I stare at them." My friend said, "I don't know if the person wants to be helped or not." I just said, "You could ask!" This person is an intelligent, with-it person but it did not cross her mind to ask.

Sharon: I think this is a theological issue. We are taught not to ask. We are taught what respect is. A pretty weird version of respect. We are taught what is okay in the church.

Christine: And not just in the church. Sometimes people say, "I am afraid to ask because they might bite my head off." I ask, "Has anyone ever done that to you?" And they say, "No but I am afraid someone will." I don't understand their fear.

Gail: Or they will say, "Can I ask you something? Did you have polio?" "No." "Oh I am sorry." "I have cerebral palsy" and I give a ten-second definition. Then they apologize and I feel bad I don't have polio. That ends the conversation. They are brave enough to ask the first question so why can't they listen and learn something about CP?

Christine: People don't ever ask me. There was this professor that I worked with for two years. One day he and my dad were out jogging and he asked my dad, "Did she have a stroke?"

Joan: People assume that we are all supposed to be the same. It is like the question, "What do women think about this?" Now it is "What do the disabled think of this?"

Liz: I wonder if people do not ask because what we say is something they might not want to hear. Silence is better than hearing.

Christine: We are supposed to make them feel okay.

Elinor: What strategies can we use to change this? We need short, maybe written, descriptions of our particular situation. It needs to be short. Some people close down very quickly or write you off as making excuses. I'm not willing to say it again and again. I tell people once and expect them to know. But then I sometimes have to tell myself every day! That's my reality; I would rather not know either. It has probably happened with my children. I told them once, about four years ago. They might need to hear it again, or to know something else, or to be updated.

Joan: What is our responsibility regarding educating others? We have to educate our doctors, and medical professionals, our classmates ...

Gail: It never stops.

Christine: Yes, we are always meeting new people. Now I am going into a new phase of my life. I am going to meet people who do not know about my abilities and limitations. But I usually just go on with my life and don't explain my disabilities. I probably should. People have questions they never had courage to ask.

Joan: Or people will ask others, "What's wrong with Christine?"

Christine: Yes, and some people will know that I have CP but no one will try to understand my situation if they do not talk with me about it.

Gail: Sometimes they will make up information. For example, when I was moving into ministry, I was settled into a congregation by the church. Before I moved, people there heard I was disabled. Some people thought I had multiple sclerosis. Someone's relative had MS and was using a wheelchair. So the word got around before I got there that I used a wheelchair. And they had a four-level house for me to live in. Pretty soon somebody else knew somebody who had died with MS. So I was practically dead before I got there. I asked for my personnel file when I moved to Saskatchewan and wrote in it what I wanted to have there.

Christine: It never ends.

Joan: It takes energy.

Gail: I once met a doctor who asked me to do a video for educating people. When I went to the lab to do the video, I was asked, "Who is your doctor? What surgery are you here for?" I had come to do an educational video that could be used to tell people about CP. But they just couldn't get it. They thought they were going to fix me. There was no thought that a recipient of services could do the educating.

Elinor: Some people are afraid to become friends because they are afraid of what they will be asked to do. And sometimes I am afraid I will be asked more than I can give.

Gail: Yes, when I was in school I had to use crutches. I actually was told later, "We did not want to be bothered about you." I was too much trouble.

Elinor: There's a lack of understanding of things that are chronic, that don't get better. Or people associate assisting you with preventing your becoming independent.

Christine: People seem to get tired of helping. They seem to wonder, "What have I been doing all this for?" if she is not going to get better.

Joan: I had no needles for diabetes for six months after my child, Nicholas, was born. It is common for women who are nursing not to have to take insulin. Someone asked me how long I was going to keep nursing him. I said until he was 24! They said, "But maybe you won't have to go on insulin again. You have been off for so long." But I knew I would have to go back on. They were silencing me, trying to keep me from saying what was true, in order to comfort me.

Liz: I have been symptom free for a while now. Some people say, "Maybe you never had multiple sclerosis" or "Perhaps now you've grown through that." The standard is always measured by the days that are symptom free. The days with symptoms are never taken as the norm. But I am me on days with or without symptoms. Even someone close once said, "You would never know there is anything wrong with you."

Christine: Or they say, "You hide it well."

Gail: Do you notice a difference in how people treat you? They say things to me they wouldn't say to someone else, like telling me I'm too much trouble. Or they also tell me things about themselves that they wouldn't tell others. People want to tell you about every ailment they ever had.

Joan: That is right! Or they want to tell you about some friend of theirs who had the same disability as you. Then they end their story by saying, "And she died." How the heck is that supposed to make you feel?

Jayne: I was in hospital with depression. An acquaint-
            ance from a writer's group came to visit me. He
            was talking, and said, "My sister-in-law was
            depressed for 25 years and then she killed her-
            self." I was really upset. I'd been depressed for
            almost 25 years. What a ridiculous thing to say!

Elinor: Sometimes I have to protect myself from becom-
            ing a caregiver. People come to be helpful and I
            end up taking care of them. Sometimes I revel in it
            and sometimes, it is beyond what is healthy for
            me. It has to do with learning and respecting my
            own limitations. I started to say no to some peo-
            ple.

Liz: There's another area we have not touched on and
            that is technology. Or people's attitudes about
            technology. Why is it that using technological aids
            to daily living is seen as taking the easy way out, a
            sign of falling from human grace, inappropriate for
            someone your age, or a weakness? Or that you are
            lazy? The same able-bodied people who make
            these criticisms have no discomfort using an
            electric can opener or a motorized golf cart.

Christine: If people can see a purpose, it seems to be okay.
            Once when I had a cast, I got lots of attention. It
            was seen as temporary and gave me a certain
            status. But it was not okay to be disabled over the
            long term.

Liz: And we are not supposed to be able to choose.
            For example, to use canes outdoors, then hold
            onto furniture instead of using canes to get around
            the house. It is seen as inconsistent to use a cane
            sometimes and not at others.

Sharon: Or people ask me why I use a scooter.

Liz: Or why we park the scooter and use canes. I have been accused of being lazy or abusing people's sympathy. Using a scooter is seen to be dishonest if we really do not "need" the scooter. If you can use the canes, then why use a scooter?

Christine: When you're born with CP, the goal is to walk unaided, or with canes. It is failure to use a wheelchair. I was born with CP. They discovered it early and so I was put into physiotherapy. The whole goal of physiotherapy was to get me to walk.

Gail: I've been going to physiotherapy for 50 years and I'm not "better" yet!

Sharon: There are all kinds of comments. Some people say, "I wish I could use that kind of thing."

Gail: I would say, "Any time you want to trade places, you can take my taxis and scooters any time!" And pay for them!

Liz: We have not talked about economics and jobs. Society recognizes employment in certain ways. Discrimination occurs.

Christine: There was a job opening at a camp for disabled children. I applied two different times to that camp. Both times they asked me, "Do you have any physical limitations?" I thought this camp for children with disabilities would be a safe and accepting environment. So I told them I had CP, thinking for once in my life it would be a bonus to my getting a job. But it was a detriment not a bonus. They focused completely on what I could not do, for example, I'm not able to push a wheelchair. In a camp counsellor position, that's only one aspect of the job. If that's what they want, they should get body builders. My disability was not an asset. They wanted to hire others with more strength than me.

Gail: Another thing is how costly some of the equipment is. And how demeaning it is to go for equipment. I would not go through the bureaucracy of fifteen requisitions to get something I needed for free. Instead I paid over $70 for a small grab bar. A friend of mine needed to get her walker repaired. At the repair place, it costs $30 per wheel. She could have gone to Canadian Tire and paid $5 per wheel but she did not have the energy to be able to do that.

Elinor: I made the choice, partly for health reasons, to be at home when our children were small. When I became disabled, I had no disability insurance. That affected our potential income. This issue became more acute when Rob died. I have needed to ask for help from others.

Sharon: The whole move related to health-care cutbacks is terrorizing. Some of us are on pension schemes so we can get 80% of many costs back. But even 20% of drugs is a huge amount.

Charlotte: Part of the reason that Barb had money when she died was that many long-term, health-care institutions will not take people on oxygen and so there was the possibility that she would have to hire an attendant to care for her. She lived very frugally in order to have sufficient funds to cover long-term, health-care needs.

Joan: We are supposed to be thankful that we get coverage. But why should any of us have to pay for what we need to live?

Jayne: It also traps people on social assistance who have needs.

Liz: And the working poor who do not have benefits, especially if they are part-time or on minimum wage. The costs are prohibitive. You cannot afford to get sick if you are on a low income.

Elinor: So many chronic conditions are made more extreme by stress. Financial stress is right up there.

Sharon: Abuse of people with disabilities is common. Then there is fear of economics: fear of losing your job, of losing financial security in the workplace.

Joan: There is abuse in homes. It is terrible, and brings so much fear. Sometimes even when caregivers abuse, people are still "grateful" for any help they get.

Jayne: I have to work not to get overcome by bitterness. Not having enough money and energy drains me. Then I am more depressed. Then I have less energy and can't get a job that allows me flexibility and enough income. So I stay on social assistance which is better than nothing but not enough. And there's never a day off.

It is a cycle: you hurt and so you are seen as bad and so you hurt. Therefore you are poor, therefore you are angry, and you are hurt. It is hard not giving up on the whole damned world. It is always hard.

Liz: There is never a day off!

Jayne: And then people say, "It is so good you are not angry and bitter." Shit! It is more than just gratitude that I need. It is not being demeaned again and again.

Liz: Humiliation is so painful for me.

Christine: Not just for you!

Liz: When I am hurt by humiliation, I get angry. Other times I just get totally wiped out by it. I feel silenced. Breaking the cycle of anger involves breaking the cycle of humiliation. In the first five years that I had MS, I had to change my body image. My self-esteem plummeted because everything that was "conspicuous" was too humiliating. There are a variety of things that I feel humiliated by, although there are fewer in the last five years than in the first five years. The last five years, I've had more experience so it doesn't seem as painful.

Gail: Women are taught to be inconspicuous and decorative. Taught to be silent and invisible.

Jayne: We are poor sex objects if we are disabled.

Liz: Interesting that we have not talked about sex.

Gail: People assumed that our children were adopted. When we took our son in to be tested for learning disabilities the doctors all assumed he was adopted.

Joan: That may explain why men drop a woman when they find out she has a disability.

Christine: I have only known one man who liked all of me. Not that he focused on my disability, but he accepted it. He liked to touch my hand. I expect future relationships to be like that. I can't be with someone who ignores it or is ashamed of my disabled hand.

Joan: I think that one of the messages society gives us is that we should be thankful for the attention we get. So society says, "Christine, you should be thankful that someone wants to be in relationship with you, even if they only want to be in relationship with part of you." I am so tired of this grateful crap! And I get angry, and it takes so much energy to be angry.

Sharon: There is a sense of anger in surviving.

Joan: Sometimes I am angry at my body. Sometimes I am angry at myself.

Sharon: I get angry at myself for how I am unable to do or not do things. I am not able to differentiate between the things I should have to deal with or just are part of the disability. Sometimes I am angry at just having to get up and get dressed.

Gail: It takes so much energy just to get from one place to the other. There has to be a heaven with no physical barriers.

Liz: We have learned to deal with anger in so many ways so that we can be safe, so that people will care for us and be around us. Does that silence others? When I first had MS, I was trying to learn about it and I was very angry. But the message I heard was, "Don't be angry around us." When I first went to the MS support group, I found myself wanting to leave. The loudest and clearest message I got was that other people feel it is not safe to be angry. We need to talk about and strategize about anger.

Joan: This is the first time I have been with a community of women with disabilities and chronic illnesses where anger has been so freely discussed.

Sharon: We are here to talk about the gut stuff and to gather wisdom from it. I have never been in a group where anger is discussed.

Christine: In our society you cannot be angry. People say,

"Forget it! Get on with your life."

Sharon: And yet we live our lives in the most violent of times.

Christine: People are always trying to suppress anger, their own or someone else's. But anger can be used in positive ways. Anger helps you change unjust systems, shows you what needs to be changed. People need to know that it is okay to feel angry.

Elinor: Sometimes the anger just needs to be expressed. But when some people feel I am angry with them, they get frightened. They feel like we are going to be angry forever, or cry forever. I have tried but I can't. It is important to have permission to be angry as long as I need to be angry, to cry as long as I need to cry. Then I can do something else. Then I can act or let go of the anger and energy.

Joan: I wonder if the church is nowhere in terms of anger. I wonder if the church does not want to hear our anger.

Liz: Especially when it is directed at them and a theology that says, "Don't be angry."

Joan: It's even worse for women because women aren't supposed to get angry.

I get really angry when I think people do not understand me. Even sometimes in a group of women, there is still a lack of understanding. We can learn but we never really understand. We have to check things out each time we meet because our needs connected to our disabilities change. For instance, sometimes I have really good control of my diabetes and can have quite a bit of flexibility in terms of what I eat. Other times, even if I am fifteen minutes late in eating,

I am in big trouble.

Elinor: Even people who have fibromyalgia have different personalities, different ways of dealing with it, and the severity of the symptoms may vary from day to day or week to week. Everyone is confused!

Part of Barb's ability to live creatively with illness was her orderliness and clear thinking. I'm not sure whether those were skills she developed or whether she was always like that!

Charlotte: For me it is not always easy to go out. I do not know what will be in some places I go to that will bother me. A friend thinks I should go out more, but it's more comfortable to be at home. Is it because of my personality, or because of my disability, that I'm more comfortable in my own home?

Elinor: And I do not travel easily. I need safety in my environment. Sometimes people perceive that as my being aloof or not wanting to be involved, but I just can't.

Joan: I am really open in telling people about my diabetes. But in fact I am a really open person. I talk to strangers, to anybody and tend to tell people who I am as a person. This has nothing to do with my diabetes. It is just who I am. I sometimes attribute things to people with disabilities that have nothing to do with their disability.

Gail: My friend sees me as a "stirrer of the pot." She thinks I say too much and push too hard. She is quiet and does not get into so much trouble. Sometimes I wish I could be like her but then I think it would be boring.

Christine: People's attitudes have also shaped my personality.

Jayne: I was recently at a Wellness Conference. A woman who used a wheelchair was speaking about her needs. It became clear that the service providers had no idea what she needed and it had not crossed their minds that she could live alone if she needed a wheelchair.

Liz: If both the fields of medicine and psychology/counselling/therapy would see disability or illness as a part of the reality of the human condition rather than a symptom of people/families over-come by the stress of living, then wisdom could be shared with no judgement or humiliation. When disability or chronic illness is seen only as a symptom of some underlying malfunction in our ability to be human, there is set up an over-against dynamic between those people with disabilities and those who make their career (I mean their living) caring for such people. Lost is the wisdom of experience for all concerned.

Elinor: Communication—really hearing—is a hard one. We always have to be checking with people and be willing to take the risk that someone won't like us. We are afraid to ask if they need assistance. But if they get mad at us for asking, so what? Are we so afraid to ask because we so much want to be liked?

Gail: The "afraid-to-ask" phenomenon is a disability too.

Joan: We are so caught up with the idea of being self-sufficient persons.

Elinor: My needs shift from day to day. My vision is that I could say, "This is how it is for me today." People say, "She is so preoccupied with her body" but it only takes minutes for me to say, "This is how I am

today and this is what I need today." Then the
next day maybe I can do it myself. But when I say
this and then they see me doing it the next day,
they think I am unreliable, and in fact, I feel
unreliable.

Joan: And the pension companies agree. They want you
to be the same all the time. And then they don't
give you a very big pension anyway. Someone
said they thought they would like to work a few
years and then get a chronic illness so that they
would get a good disability pension. It was unbe-
lievable. They would want this! There is a total
lack of understanding about what it is like to live
with chronic illness.

Charlotte: And they don't know much about disability pen-
sions!

Gail: Education needs to go on all the time. I don't think
we'll reach a place where people understand.
Disability is too threatening. Unless we can keep
all the kids learning.
                    I often am asked to do educational talks in
schools with children. I call my cane Caspar and
talk about it with the children. I tell them about
how Caspar helps me to get around. One day after
I had been with the kids, one little girl came up to
me and hugged my leg and said, "I love you."
Children get the message.

Christine: Kids are very curious about the differences in
people. But adults teach them not to ask questions
of people with disabilities. Many children ask me,
"Why is your hand like that?" I am always happy
to tell them, but sometimes, before I have a
chance to answer, an adult will tell the child
something like, "Because she's different, and that's

okay." When this happens, I feel like the child has been cheated out of a satisfactory answer. Adults should not try to silence those questions they find uncomfortable to deal with. Kids want to know why things are as they are. They are very good at accepting the differences in a person once they understand why the person is different.

Elinor: People with disabilities are seen as trouble makers if they are too articulate. What is seen as a strength in able-bodied people is seen as too articulate in a person with a disability. It's so frightening that people back up, "I'm impressed that you can speak up for yourself." They seem to think that if you can be that articulate about your needs, then you don't need whatever it is you are asking for. One of the things I am learning is to listen to my body and to say what I need.

Charlotte: For many people, especially liberal Protestants, there seems to be the idea that if you have said something, then you have done something. For Protestants, the Word is everything. But in fact, articulating the need does not mean the need is met. There has to be action.

Gail: Being able to articulate is an ability, but if you are disabled, then ALL of you is seen to be disabled. Being articulate and being disabled do not go together, at least in the minds of some able-bodied people. So they tend to dismiss you or make up something that seems to fit.

I remember my first appointment with a reha-bilitation doctor in Saskatchewan. The referral clearly said I was the United Church minister in Yellow Grass but the specialist greeted me with the words, "You're the wife of the United Church minister in Yellow Grass." It was a statement not a question.

Jayne: I am always giving people permission to ask all the questions they have. I live by a set of rules. One of the rules is that the only dumb question is the one you have not asked yet. Being willing to answer others' questions is an affirmation. And I am willing to educate anyone who wants to learn, but I don't waste time on people who don't want to know. I can only educate curious people.

Joan: We should get T-shirts made with signs: "Ask me about diabetes," "Ask me about fibromyalgia."

Elinor: I need to go back to what was said before. It is a point about language. We have been talking about language this weekend so I need to raise the concern about the way we use "dumb" because it has been used so much in our history for people who can not speak. I notice how we use it.

Jayne: It has also been used often for the silencing of people who can speak by telling them that theirs is a dumb question. We need to be careful however the silencing happens.

Elinor: There can be both articulation and silence. It is a question of power. It is choosing when to speak and when not to speak. In some situations I know I will not make myself vulnerable again.

Charlotte: That choice is so important. We do not have to say or do everything!

Joan: And we need the freedom not to feel guilty for not doing things today. I do not need to do everything every day. There are other women who are working on the same things I am. I am not alone.

Jayne: Carolyn McDade's song is so important to me.
            "No woman is required to build the world by
            destroying herself."[61] I play that song over and
            over.

Joan: My friend, Brenda, made a banner for me with
            those words on it. It came in the mail one day
            when I was dealing with awful sexism. It is impor-
            tant to me. It is important to me as well to have a
            vision of health. I really like Elinor's vision, "A
            healthy family takes sickness in stride."

Jayne: After I had my hysterectomy operation, I wanted
            to go to church but the only way I could do it was
            to lie on the floor in the minster's office and listen
            to the service. I could not stand up and I needed
            to reserve my energy so that I could go to coffee
            after the service and connect with people. I would
            have had no energy if I had had to do more than
            that. What would happen if we all were allowed
            to be in church in whatever way we could be
            there? There is the story in the Bible of the man
            whose friends let him down on his cot through the
            roof of the building so he could get to Jesus. What
            would happen if we allowed cots in our cathe-
            drals?

Gail: Part of your story was that you were going to get
            better. And it shows how accommodating the
            church is, "If that's what you needed" but just for a
            short period of time.

Jayne: When I made the suggestion to have cots in
            church, they said, "People wouldn't use them.
            They wouldn't want to be conspicuous," which
            really means "we don't want to see them." I think
            there was a feeling that the people who could
            stand and sit would be uncomfortable. It reminds

me of Christine's story about wanting to be Mary in the Nativity play.

Gail: When I was a student minister there was a lectern and a pulpit and the ministers always walked across the front of the church from one to the other at the time of the sermon. After I had been there for a few weeks doing this, my supervisor said to me that I did not have to walk across from one place to the other. I said very clearly that I was not willing to stop doing it because someone was uncomfortable seeing me do it.

Charlotte: Imagine living in a society where we can do what we want to do: lie down in church, walk across the front of the church or not, whatever we needed to do for our own well-being.

Jayne: And that everyone would see that people with disabilities provide a gift to all people. We often have no choice. If I could not lie on the floor, I could not be present. There was no choice. I have to be open about my needs for my own safety. This means we can be catalysts to bring about changes that would help everybody, would make everybody more comfortable.

Gail: You were able to choose to be there and to be clear about your needs. But many people have no choices. Or feel they have no choices. Many people simply would not have been there. They cannot even imagine any other way.

Jayne: Once when I was under suicide supervision I went to Ottawa as a guest speaker at a conference. I had it all organized so that I would have people with me at the workshops I was attending and asked people to stay with me all the time. Then I came back to the hospital. I just had to ask people and they were there.

Joan: It will be wonderful when we don't even have to ask. People would just know what we need. People would know that if I start to shake that I need a glass of juice.

Jayne: Or if they did not know what you needed they would know to ask you what you needed.
Imagine a society where people could ask for what they need.

Joan: Beyond comprehension!

Charlotte: The things that we need would be there so that our lives would be convenient.

Joan: So that you could get the laundry detergent you need.

Charlotte: I'd be considered a valued customer. I asked to order a case of the brand of laundry soap I had been using but they said it wasn't manufactured any more. So I'm experimenting. I have to buy a box and then discover my shirt gives me hives, or I can't breathe because of the scent of my pillow-case. Why do there have to be forty-two scents and fifty-three ingredients that don't matter? No one needs that. But I'm not a valued customer. One case doesn't count.

Joan: As a political act we could all use only the brand of detergent that Charlotte can use. As soon as she found the right one an alert bulletin would go out to Winnipeg and Ottawa and Fort McMurray and we would all tell all our friends to only use this brand. That is my vision of solidarity.

Elinor: And if everyone ate like Charlotte and I do the

world would be a much healthier place. Everyone would have whole foods with as little processing and additives as possible. We have been taught to think additives make food real. What an abberation!

Jayne: Not long ago, the radio reported that chickens would be dipped in trisodium phosphate to prevent salmonella contamination. That's the stuff I use to wash my walls before painting. And that ingredient will never show up on the label. What does that do for a "safe" food like chicken?

Joan: It would be great if we did not even have to call the companies to complain about the chickens or the additives or the detergent. One customer writing to say they need this for their health and well-being would be enough. Companies would not just focus on profit but would ask, What is the caring, compassionate thing to do?

　　What I want is to hold onto those visions and not just to get caught in saying that the company would not do it.

Jayne: Do we want to say anything more about laundry soap, chickens, or churches?

Joan: After a worship service, there was to be a congregational meeting. People wanted to have it right after the service, to go on without a break. My partner said no, Joan has to eat. I was glad he said it. They said that I could just bring a snack to make it easier for other people. We cannot always do just what is convenient. Lots of people have the same needs, not just me. Many elderly people and children need to eat at the proper times. It is so easy to get guilted out.

Elinor: I am thinking about what Barb once said about living in a time when women need to learn a theology of assertiveness and men of relinquishment. We were saying that women with disabilities are perceived differently. There may be different truths that we need as women with disabilities. Our needs differ. But in our society women are punished for being articulate simply because they are women.

Joan: I was at an event. Several men were going on and on about something the female speaker had said. I finally got up and said that I thought it was time a few women spoke and that the men were talking too much about this particular issues which affected women's lives. I said, "I wish men would just shut up." Three men got up and spoke as soon as I sat down. I should have said, "Thanks for proving my point."

Gail: There is such a gap between what we profess and the way we treat "the unfortunate." Such a gap between the theory and what we do. People will say they are inclusive but when they get up to speak they are not. And they do not even notice. They will say, "All brothers and sisters are welcome" except those who cannot make it up the stairs. People can be shunned or included.

Jayne: The choir at the church in Edgeley is very important. There is a man in the choir who no longer has the ability to learn new music. Sometimes therefore they sing pieces from another century. But the spirit is right to include this man. Another place will come for balance. I hate the music but love the inclusion. We always need to ask Barb's questions about who this will include and who it will leave out.

Joan: I cannot just leave out men. But I get so angry with their litany: I cannot get into the RCMP, I cannot get this job or that because I am a white male.

Charlotte: The hierarchies of gender, race, class and disability are complex for many of us. There are certainly many white men accustomed to living with privilege who are very angry about affirmative action and equality.

Joan: Barb addressed that question when she talked about liberalism and asked about who benefits.

Charlotte: We have to keep asking those questions, and keep working away to change the systems until the needs of all people who do not usually get a share in decision-making are considered in decisions.

Elinor: I envision a community or church being more creative about involving people who are unable to do the things the church usually does. For instance, I cannot go to meetings or be on committees easily because I cannot commit to regular participation. But when people invite me to become involved, they ask me to go on a committee. I cannot but that does not mean I do not have anything to offer. After being in the hospital I was asked to make a list of ways the church could be helpful to me. I included on that list that I needed to be able to give something. At the time there was not opportunity for me to be heard and as I look back, I know I withdrew further.

Joan: The church could imagine different ways of doing and being that would provide more inclusion.

Gail: More than just inclusion in Sunday morning services. More creativity in making contributions.

Charlotte: Maybe actually meeting some of our spiritual needs as women with chronic illnesses and disabilities!

Jayne: We are doing church this morning. I looked forward to this morning and being real with all of you much more than I look forward to most Sunday mornings. We are church.

We've Learned a Lot

Our lives in relationship are our teachers. As we reflected on our lives and listened to each other, we have been able been able to generate new understandings. In this chapter, we share these learnings and some strategies for living our lives.

Self-esteem

Keeping strong self-esteem challenges women with disabilities. Knowing we are loved and loveable pushes us. Without self-esteem we destroy ourselves. If we do not value ourselves, we do not take care of ourselves. We need to be attentive to our body-selves and our mental well-being. Often we have been taught that we are unacceptable and that our problems are our fault. Frequently we have experienced situations in which we are demeaned and humiliated. If our needs vary from day to day, we are viewed as unreliable. If our disabilities or illnesses are not clearly visible, we are seen as imposters.

> In a world that measures by externals, meting out what little care may be found on the basis of who looks the

worst, persons with invisible disabilities wage a constant fight to be acknowledged as less than they appear to be— an ironic war in which to be a tired and desperate foot soldier.[62]

For many women with disabilities and chronic illnesses, shame becomes a way of life. Debra Connors adds that discrimination grows out of sexism, able-ism, as well as being based on our race, age, and sexual preference. "Objectified as women and as medical, social work, and charity cases, disabled women have been deeply invalidated as human beings. We have been disabled by our society."[63] We may push us to overcompensate. Defined as less than full people, we do more than others to appear "normal."

As well, those of us who live with unpredictable chronic illnesses receive encouragement to define ourselves based on a symptom-free or "healthy" self. Symptom-free days, those days when we feel good, are named as the norm for people with chronic illnesses; we measure ourselves against an ideal state of health. In reality, symptom-filled days set our norm; for most of us, they occur more frequently than days when our symptoms do not dominate.

Our public lives also need to be respected if we are to live with strong self-esteem. Whether in our work places, our spiritual communities, or feminist gatherings, it is often assumed we will be spectators, not full participants or leaders. When we have leadership roles, people often perceive us as less or more than other humans. We may be seen as incompetent even though those things which we cannot do have no bearing on our roles and duties. Competent preachers or teachers who sit instead of stand may be seen as less than able. Or people may attribute heroic qualities that make us larger than life. Because we can preach or teach even though we have a disability, we are almost divine! High-profile people with chronic illnesses and disabilities may be expected to cope better and achieve more than our colleagues. Either way, we are not ordinary human beings with the foibles and gifts that make us who we are as persons.

Part of self-esteem requires being agents of our own lives, that is, seeing ourselves as actors and participants in our own destinies, making choices about how we will live our lives. In our society, because of social discrimination and lack of access, women with disabilities and chronic illnesses often have fewer choices than those who are able-bodied. The choices that we can make are important to us. We want to be part of the whole of society and to participate in the naming and shaping of the common good.

People without disabilities and chronic illnesses need to listen to our needs and take seriously the realities of our lives. Our experience shows that often people with power and able bodies and minds want us to take care of them emotionally. They want us to educate them about our needs and remind them of those needs so that they do not have to remember them. Usually they want us to get well and often get irritated when we do not.

We do not have energy to do other people's work as well as concentrate on our own survival and well-being. Most of us live with a chronic level of exhaustion from lack of access, from needing to watch out for dangers to our existence, from dealing with other people's reactions to us, as well as the fact that our bodies often seem to betray us. As Elizabeth O'Connor says, " ... when one is ill the illness becomes one's work. When we ask a patient how [s]he feels we are asking [her] him to talk about [her] his work."[64] Or as Elinor says, "It takes a lot of ability to live with disability!" We need reinforcement for our ability, acknowledgment that part of our work is living with disabilities and chronic illnesses. The onus lies with people who are able to learn about and accommodate the members of their group and community who do not live with bodily and mental privilege. We want to live in a world where the burden of responsibility is on the privileged. We want those who pay less of the personal and economic cost of life in a disabling society to be accountable, and we are not willing to let them off the hook.

Theologically this may mean that those with disabilities create a theology of assertiveness and those who are able-bodied practise theology of relinquishment. Not everyone comes to truth in the same way. Those who have power may need to relinquish some of their power and explore what life is like when there is little or less privilege in order to be in solidarity and to be advocates. Those with disabilities and chronic illnesses who have not been heard in systems of power may need to be assertive, to name their needs clearly and strongly to demand just systems. Truth comes out of interaction; justice demands solidarity and commitment to the least powerful.

To have self-esteem means that "no woman is required to build the world by destroying herself." It means taking care of ourselves, recognizing that we have the right to be as we are, to have a place in society and power to make decisions about our own lives. To have self-esteem means having the freedom to define the norm for life as something other than the ideal of perfection: perfect health, perfect body image, perfect mobility. It means having our boundaries respected, living without violence, in positive (sometimes sexual) relationships. It demands that we be viewed realistically as ordinary human beings, not more or less than others around us. It asks that other people take care not to offend and lay extra burdens on us. It means assertiveness in community. It means valuing our lives, ourselves, our wisdom.

Knowing Our Bodies

We know more about our own bodies than anybody else does. Yet we often do not receive credit for what we know about our bodies. Medical practitioners do not acknowledge some of our conditions nor the extent to which these conditions affect our lives. Many doctors want us to get well; our continuing problems become symbols of "their failure" to make us well. Misdiagnosis is common. Fragmented services without a holistic approach present special problems for those of us with multiple disabilities. We need adequate medical care, aids to living, and economic viability.

The costliness of equipment and drugs and the lack of insurance available for persons with pre-existing conditions create serious problems. For those of us on social assistance, the continual process of having to prove that we are still disabled frustrates us repeatedly.

As well as our medical and economic needs, we need safety. For those of us with uncertain mobility, safety means being able to have the assistance of an arm to hold, or space for us to use canes, walkers, wheelchairs or scooters. Safety involves streets, ramps, hallways, and washrooms that are even and unobstructed. It requires adequate lighting so that we do not become more vulnerable by dark places from which we cannot easily escape. All of us who live with disabilities and chronic illnesses have particular needs for our safety and well-being based on our specific conditions. Our physical safety often engulfs us as a primary focus. Many of us have to know what our environment will be like before we go somewhere in order to have the assurance that our bodies will be able to cope. Risks always exist, but we prefer to measure some of those risks as we decide whether to participate in something rather than being thrust into what proves to be a dangerous environment for us.

For those of us who live with mental illnesses, safety constitutes an extremely important matter. Some of us live with the consequences of having had unsafe childhoods and now in adulthood, we need safe spaces where we don't feel overwhelmed.

All of us need both physical and emotional safety. Starhawk helpfully writes that "Safety in a group is not a matter of niceness or politeness." She elaborates noting that when we are expected to be nice, we do not feel safe enough to expose the deeper parts of ourselves that might not seem so nice. While groups always hold some risks, they can work to share the risks, to name the boundaries and power structures, and to eliminate hidden agendas. When the whole groups shares the risks, "we can face them with solidarity. Solidarity is based on the principle that we are willing to put ourselves at risk to protect each other."[65]

Because our bodies are the centres of our political struggles, we need communities of friends (and ideally, a society) that live in solidarity with us.

Our knowledge of our bodies also means that most of us fine tune organizational and planning skills. We plan our days around our eating and rest needs, or around how we will get to the places we need or want to be. Kathy Charmaz notes, "The problems with which ill people struggle are existential; their solutions are often organizational."[66] Often those of us who are chronically ill develop routines that help us manage or mask our symptoms. Organizing the day may become a consuming interest. And although we wish there were respite care for us, we never get a day off.

Losses and Grief

All of us have experienced losses because we are disabled or chronically ill.

For some of us, becoming chronically ill in later life meant loss of our self-image and our understanding of who we are and what we can do in this world. For some of us, our illnesses meant loss of the intimate relationships that once sustained us. For some of us, our disabilities contributed to lack of access to the education, employment or relationships we wanted, and so we have experienced the loss of dreams or hope. All of us have lost the ability to take things for granted. Often we want to find hope but in fact, despair prevails. We lose hope at certain points in our lives when we cannot see a future for ourselves.

We need to express grief over our losses. Sometimes we feel like an embodiment of grief. As the Collective was working on this project Joan's father became ill. She wrote,

> My dad is sick and getting worse instead of better. He has a virus in his brain, and because it is a virus there is nothing they can do. Some people get better fairly quickly, some take longer, and some never recover. He is very confused and has trouble with simple tasks. He cannot be left alone.
>
> I feel like I have lost my dad and I do not know when or if he is coming back.
>
> As I think about it, it seems to me that grief over my dad is something like the grief I sometimes feel over

178 Not All Violins

having diabetes. Sometimes it sweeps over me like a
wave until I feel like I might drown. Other times the tide
goes in and out and I feel like I will be okay for a while.

People who experience disabilities and chronic illnesses frequently
go though the stages of grief as described by Elizabeth Kubler
Ross: denial/shock, anger, bargaining, depression/letting go,
acceptance/re-establishment.[67] These stages come in varying
intensity depending on what has happened to us, how it disrupts
our lives, and how much support we have as we live through the
uncertainty created by sudden illness or disability. The stages last
different lengths of time for different people. There is no "right
way" to do grief. We simply live with it, embody it in different
ways at different points as our lives go on. It does not go away. If
we could give a gift to all people with disabilities and chronic
illnesses it would be permission to feel anger and grief, and to
have safe spaces to explore and express the wide range of feelings
that dwell inside. Working together in this Collective has given us
new permission to speak the truth of our lives and to
acknowledge the feelings we have.

All of us have known anger through living with our disabilities
and chronic illnesses: when we dropped a plate of stew on our
freshly cleaned carpet because our hands did not work, when we
were turned down for a job, when someone made a degrading
remark to us, when medical practitioners poked and prodded as if
we were a lump of flesh and not a person, when we have not
heard part of an important conversation, or when we woke up in
the morning knowing the day would be filled with pain or inability
to do what we wanted to do. Our anger is real. Yet we do not
always have places that are safe to express our anger. Our
experience suggests that anger is not acceptable in our society,
especially from women. For women who have been part of
Christian churches, the problem of anger increases since anger
corresponds with sin rather than being accepted as a healthy
emotion that needs appropriate expression. The medical
profession has also denied women's anger by making anger a

symptom of several disorders. Thus when women who live with mental illness express anger, the anger is named as a part of the illness. Anger is also sometimes cited as a symptom of multiple sclerosis or diabetes. Sometimes our anger is trivialized by laughter and comments such as, "She must be premenstrual!" or we are drugged to prevent us from feeling the anger that lives within our bodies. The truth of our bodies and our lives must be expressed and validated. That truth includes anger. Our anger plays a part in our grief and in our will to survive and to know justice.

Many people with disabilities and chronic illnesses contend with lengthy and recurring periods of depression. When we gathered as a Collective we talked about and expressed anger. We spent less time focused on depression and yet many of us have had deep struggles with depression. During the years in which we have been working together several of us have had times of being held in its grip. When we talked together about some of the missing pieces of our life stories as we had written them, we acknowledged that this book tells of the spiritual resources that allowed us to live with some measure of grace through those periods (sometimes of several years) but does not describe the times of despair and depression, partly because we cannot bear or afford to go back into those depths on the days when we are well enough to write.

The final stage in Kubler-Ross's paradigm of grief is "acceptance." Franklin Shontz claims that "to overcome a disability means to stop thinking about it all the time and to get on with the business of living as best one can." He explains that a person has come to terms with a disability or chronic illness when "the problem of contending with it ceases to be the dominant element in that person's total psychological structure or life space."[68] While the language of "overcoming" our disabilities is not necessarily helpful (we live with them rather than conquering them in some way), Shontz's point that acceptance occurs when the disability or chronic illness does not dominate all of one's life is significant. He notes that people are very adaptive and can live with all kinds of pain, difficulties, and discomforts if they have meaning in their lives. We would add that we need physical and emotional safety as well as meaning. If we are unsafe, our bodily and psychological needs dominate. When we are safe we are free to think about other things and, as Shontz says, "get on with the business of living as best we can." For most people, reconciling ourselves to our chronic illnesses means tolerating them. It usually means establishment of a whole new life. Acceptance is active. Acceptance allows for finding new dimensions in a fulfilling life.

As we come to terms with our transformed lives, we need to know that our lives have meaning. At the consultation we discussed whether all aspects of our lives need to be meaningful and disagreed about that. Some of the Collective see suffering as having meaning or at least the potential for meaning. Others of the Collective think that suffering is inherently meaningless, that is, suffering is a random event with no more meaning than the fact that some people have brown eyes while others have green eyes. While we agree that it is important to find meaning in our lives, we are not of common mind about how to view suffering. All of us do agree that imposed pain (for example, through violence) is wrong.

One of the losses that was significant for many of us was the loss of relationships. Some of us who used to be in helping professions have lost our capacity to be helper, and have become the recipients of help. All of us notice the dilemma of maintaining relationships when so much of our time and energy is used for survival. If we do not take the initiative to maintain friendships and partnerships, we invite future isolation. There is loneliness in disability.

Relationships

Relationships centre our lives. We want to be in healthy, positive, and ongoing relationships. We also recognize that others do not always find it easy to be in relationship with us. Like us, the people whom we hold dear—friends, husbands, lovers, children—need to have spaces where they can tell the truth about their lives and their emotions. The experiences of those who live with our uncertainties, unpredictabilities, frustrations, and pain are different from our experiences of those same events. Our loved ones need support from others in similar circumstances. They deserve a safe place to deal with their anger that we are not always able to meet their needs or to be as attentive as would be appreciated. They need opportunities to talk about the feelings of guilt, fear, and hurt that exist in their lives. They have spiritual needs that differ from ours. With one another they can create and share the resources they need.

All of us have experienced frustration with people who should know better, who make errors in judgement that are hurtful to us or put us at unnecessary risk. Sometimes we think people should understand the complexities of our lives but they leave us feeling hurt or let down. We expect others to understand our bodily conditions if they love us. When we experience rejection or hurt, we tend to withdraw. We always live in hope that feminist communities and close friends will support us and allow our needs to be heard and considered in decisions. We hope that men or women who we want as friends or lovers will take us seriously. We have found, however, that we need to find people who are actually supportive, not just people who are supposed to be supportive. We know, too, that high numbers of women with disabilities and chronic illnesses are left by their partners. We need supportive and significant relationships beyond those with our immediate families because our families may or may not endure, or be able to give us the support we need.

We became clear that we must set boundaries as women with disabilities and chronic illnesses. Many able-bodied people do not respect our boundaries. In relationships they do not accept our limits. In physical settings where we need assistance, they do not ask what kind of assistance we need. People often assume we need assistance when we do not. We believe we have the right to set and maintain boundaries in relation to our personhood and our space.

We also believe that we have the right to be whole in our sexual lives. Some people assume that we are easy victims; the rate of sexual violence against women with physical and mental disabilities is significantly higher than against able women. But there is also much de-sexing of people with disabilities. For example, although Gail is married, people assume that her children are not birth children because she lives with a disability. People assume that she could not be not sexually active. Many women with disabilities and chronic illnesses experience difficulty finding sexual relationships of mutuality and respect, where the disability is simply accepted as part of the reality. Self-esteem flourishes if we have opportunities for appropriate and enjoyable sex and affection in our lives.

Bernice Fischer and Roberta Galler write about women's friendships between disabled and non-disabled women. They discovered two areas that need balance: physical help and emotional reciprocity.

> The disabled women we talked with often alluded to a sort of unspoken bargain they struck with their non-disabled friends. Recognizing that friendship requires a certain special accommodation (if not direct physical help) by non-disabled friends, the disabled woman attempted to balance the scale by being especially attentive and supportive in the emotional sphere, being extragood listeners, comforters and so forth. Such an attempt, however, needs to be understood in the context of the strong investment in physical autonomy that characterized the disabled women with whom we spoke. All of them resented being given help they did not need or want.[69]

This quality of mutuality ranks as very significant for women with differences. We need both autonomy and support in our relationships.

Many people find it hard to be in relationships of accompaniment. Our society focuses on activities, on doing, and on fixing. We cannot be fixed. We find that generally people want to do something when what we need is someone just to be near. Some want to help for a while, but usually they expect us to get better then get discouraged when we do not. Other times we experience a level of condescension when groups are pleased that they have two or three disabled participants and thus think they have dealt with "that issue."

But friendship as a political act requires taking people seriously. Margo Adair helpfully focuses the discussion of politics of relationship when she says, "We must get it out of our heads and stop judging by how it feels personally rather than what it does socially. We meet nice guys all over the place who do atrocious things. We must look deeper into where people's interests lie, not how congenial they are."[70] Sometimes entering into friendships can be the political act. Other times withdrawing from relationships that do not allow us respect and freedom with appropriate assistance may be the needed political act.

Silencing

All of us have experienced social silencing. We have been actively discouraged from talking about our lives, about the pain, the frustration, the anger, and the lack of resources and access that confront us. We have been told that there is always somebody who is worse off and that we should be grateful for not being in any worse shape than we are. This extends a powerful tool for social silencing. It minimizes us and does not allow us to experience our own experiences fully.

This habit of minimizing our lives as women with disabilities and chronic illnesses seems to us a form of clutching at superiority by people who have not yet had to deal with bodily betrayals and malfunctions. Ironically, unlike other prejudices where differences of race or gender are permanent features, disability can happen to anyone. All of us are likely to live with temporary or long-term disabilities at some point in our lives. To be silenced, or to be seen as problems to be fixed, is not helpful. Hearing voices and experiences of people with disabilities and chronic illnesses can influence our social consciousness so that medical, technological, and social supports systems will deal adequately with what happens to almost all of us sooner or later. We need to learn from those who know how to deal with disabilities and chronic illnesses from long experience. Voices that would provide teaching for life should not be silenced.

Liz's decision to tell one person each day about what life is really like offers a good strategy to prevent silencing and slowly to bring others on board.

Silencing also comes for articulate women with disabilities. Generally, being articulate is seen as an asset in our society, but for women with disabilities, it seems a drawback. We are seen as troublemakers if we know how to question what is being done to us medically or socially, if we say what we think and experience. Most people prefer that we remain silent except when expressing gratitude. The thought seems to be that if you can articulate your needs then you can meet them. Assertiveness and expression may be one step in getting one's needs met, but articulation is not sufficient and not all people with disabilities have voice or capacity to articulate and advocate for their own needs.

We also recognize that sometimes we choose silence. In some situations we feel too vulnerable to speak or to make our needs known. Our safety and well-being require higher priority than educating others towards justice. Many times we choose silence because it takes too much energy to make ourselves vulnerable to the hurt, humiliation, or damage that others can bring on us.

Laughter

We in the Barb Wire Collective also believe that humour can be a healing force in this broken world. When we laugh together, we create bonds that are deep and strong. We believe that humour grows out of concrete situations and lifts people up rather than putting them down. Jokes that injure and humiliate are not humorous. As we gathered to prepare this book, our laughter rang out. All of us expressed anger at the outrageous injustice of the world and found grace through the moments of seeing the absurd and creating alternate scenarios to hurtful situations we had experienced. We wondered often how the smartest people can manage to say the most ridiculous things. Being part of a group that shares the common experience of being degraded and devalued by society means we can share stories that are instantly recognizable to all of us. Even though our disabilities and chronic illnesses vary, our treatment by others and by society in general is remarkably similar. And when we come together we can transform the painful, showing it in all its absurdity, laughing at the gruesome without having to explain why it strikes us as funny. Just as anger creates a bond and motivates us to work for justice, laughter draws us together and empowers and energizes us to work for change in the world.

Conclusions

Reflection on our experiences has enabled us to get new insights into life as women with disabilities and chronic illnesses.

We know that self-esteem is important. We need to take care of ourselves, to recognize that we have the right to be as we are, and to make decisions about our own lives. To have self-esteem means having freedom: freedom from bodily ideals, from physical and social dangers; freedom to live in positive relationships as ordinary people who value our lives and their meaning in this world.

We know our bodies best and we need medical and economic resources to live in our bodies viably. We have high needs for safety, and we often spend much of our time organizing and planning our lives to manage our symptoms.

All of us know losses: the loss of self image, of relationships, of dreams. Our lives often hold an ebb and flow of grief that comes in waves through the varying stages of grief. We need meaning in our lives in order to go on.

Our relationships hold great value for us. There are challenges for those with whom we share intimacy; there are disappointments when people do not understand us. We believe that physical and emotional reciprocity produce strong bonds in our relationships. We often want accompaniment instead of solutions.

We need also to tell the truth about our lives. Women with

disabilities and chronic illnesses know much social silencing. Sometimes we choose silence as a practical strategy for self-preservation or to conserve our energy.

Laughter with those who share common experiences proves to be a great healer. It allows us to create bonds, to transform the anger and pain we feel, and it energizes us towards work for change in the world.

We've learned a lot!

Visioning

Our work together leads us to the belief that we need imagination as well as articulation and daily strategies. Our visions are individual and intertwined into communal visions that have become a part of our lives. We draw energy from each other and help each other live towards our dreams.

Part of being feminist entails creating visions. It is political to have a vision and feminist spirituality is by nature a political act and political expression. Part of our function as feminists involves imagining a different way of life.

Our visions often grow out of the pain and discrimination in our own lives. We experience life in a society that does not value us as women with disabilities. We begin to envision life if society were inclusive of our lives and valuing of all people. We desire the freedom to live ordinary lives: to shop without clerks ignoring us or making rude remarks, to attend events with consideration of accessible space and appropriate environments, to be in relationships where we are loved just as we are. We need rich imaginations to create visions of what that world could be like.

At any given point we may or may not have visions. Sometimes we do not have energy to create visions or cannot see any way that looks different. Not everyone dreams with clear vision, and having visions does not mean we always live hopefully. Many times we despair. We do not always see rays of hope for a transformed world. Depression is a frequent companion. Much energy is used on survival, on keeping going in a world that is not designed for easy living.

Joan adds:

> Our visions are not just articulate and rational. They are more than that. What I conceive when I articulate in rational terms, I do not see happening in a couple of years. But in my imagination and in my dreams, these things will happen. Visions keep me going.

Sometimes we do hope; we do dream of life in all its fullness. For us this does not mean elimination of disabilities or chronic illnesses (although there are certainly days when we would gladly live without them!). Rather we conceive of a life that integrates us fully and allows us the mobility and respect to live rich and interesting lives as part of the diversity of creation.

The dialogue goes on.

Liz: I would hope a variety of approaches to making life more comfortable and fulfilling would be equally acceptable socially. As long as society has a "cure" mentality, then the search for meaning becomes devalued and is often lost. Scientific and medical research seeks understanding and continue to unlock pieces of our human experience of body, mind, and spirit. While they do this, my vision is that we could be a society that accepts the current reality that most people at some time or another in their lives experience illness or body dysfunction. It is a norm—not one we like or understand, but it does seem to be a norm of human experience. As long as illness is seen to be "abnormal" we will be unable to explore fully the experience of pain or suffering not only in our own lives but in the world.

Elinor: The time is coming and is now ... I have always valued that idea from the Bible.[71] There are changes and there have been changes. What needs to happen is already happening in seed-like ways.

For example, the Cancer Society had some community educational evenings with people practising alternative forms of medicine and healing. A hundred and fifty people showed up—people who are into massage therapy, nutritional practices, and other things. One of my visions is that there be much more interconnection between different kinds of healing, between the traditional medical practitioners and those doing alternative forms of healing. It is beginning and is happening in seed-like ways that will grow.

Maybe our children and our grandchildren will see it. It is dismally slow. But there are signs that it is happening. There is backlash so it must be growing. We need to celebrate what is. It is not enough to say when we get to heaven it will all be fine. Rather we need to ask, how are we each making that vision a reality?

Joan: We need to celebrate little victories. I find that those little celebrations help me a lot.

Jayne: Behold the turtle who only makes progress when she sticks her neck out.

Joan: What is your vision, Gail?

Gail: Thinking specifically of the physical church build-ing, my vision of accessibility has two aspects to it. First of all, all places of worship would be physically less imposing. All parts of every building would be accessible including the pulpit!

The other part of my vision is an attitude thing. I would like to get rid of the smugness and condescension that there is around having disabled people in church. Physical barriers may well have been modified but often an attitude of condescension remains.

There is a guy whose head I would like to step on. He is always asking me what I need. "Is the elevator okay? Do you need anything?" But he is so self-satisfied about the whole thing that I just want to scream.

It would be nice if we could just get on with our lives. People would not even notice when they gave the help that is needed.

Joan: They would just take it in stride.

Elinor: Or to use a wheeled image, roll with it.

Sometimes our vision is very simple. For example, as we talked about our visions Joan said that her vision is that when she is having a diabetic reaction, someone would get her something to drink: "It's not that complicated." Most of what we would like is not that complicated! It simply would require social will and deliberate choice on the part of society.

Along with our conversations and the visions integrated with our stories, three of our members wrote additional pieces.

My Vision of Life with Justice
Mary Elford

What could society be like, if justice were prevalent for women with disabilities?

I believe that we would have a strong sense of the worth and value and importance of each person. The knowledge that each one of us is a child of God, created and loved by God, is holy knowledge. If I know that I am made in God's image, I affirm my own worth. When I am able to accept that all of me is made in God's image, I come closer to realizing that all of me reflects something of God. This is especially true for the parts of me that I try to hide or ignore, my disability, my imperfections. When I accept and love myself as God's loved creation, formed to be who I am, with potential to grow into my own being, then I am freed to love others, as I come to know that they, too, resemble God and are cherished by God.

This knowledge, in my vision of what could be, would become common. In turn, each person's picture of what God is like will need to be reworked. If we can see something of God in each neighbour, God cannot be limited to a far away Spirit. If disability mirrors God's image, God must expand to include disability and weakness, as well as perfection and strength. Removing limits from our image of God imposes other limits on our perception of God's abilities.

The technology that helps to overcome a hearing disability is expensive. In this society of justice, the wealth of the disabled person would not be a factor in the help available to her. Continuing research would push at the edges of discovery in all fields, including surgery, technology, communication, causes and prevention, and public education. For instance, and this is where I'm really going to let go and dream, we will have transplants of nerves, either from someone else, or else grown from some sort of culture. We will have transplants of the part of the inner ear that is missing or defective. We will have tests that can accurately measure a baby's hearing, and corrective surgery will take place as soon as possible, so their communication will not be delayed. This surgery will be on an outpatient basis. For other people, we will have small comfortable hearing aids with a long-lasting power source. Each person would learn at least the alphabet, in American Sign Language, so that any deaf or hard of hearing person could communicate. Another part of each person's education will involve wearing ear plugs for a week, to give everyone a sense of what it is like for someone who cannot hear.

After these and any other necessary changes occur, society will be different for women with disabilities. I'd like to dream some more about how that will look.

We will notice and address the person, not the disability. Instead of first seeing the hearing aid, the wheelchair, the limp, we will see an interesting person, created in God's image, beloved of God, capable of sharing love.

We will make an effort to include those who don't quite fit, who stand on the margins. The ones on the margins will be free to choose to be included as part of the group, without fear or shame.

I will know that this new society has become a reality, on the day when I ask a tired store clerk to tell me again how much I owe, and she smiles pleasantly and answers me patiently and without condemnation.

When there is no need for anyone to clutch superiority, but all people are seen as equal and worthy, then this vision will become reality. I look for that day.

Visions
Sharon Davis

Life, Hopes, Dreams, and Visions are mine because I choose them to be. I choose them to be because of the faith and spirituality of many on this earth. I choose them because of my own personal faith and spirituality. Faith and spirituality demand of me, and I believe everyone, many things. As Rosemary Doran says:

> As a human, a woman, made in God's image.
> I must speak out about injustice,

call myself and others to responsibility,
send myself and others to serve,
challenge my family, my generation, my society to re-examine
its values,
love my neighbour—wherever, whoever, however he or she is.
Only then will the image of God in me be true, closer to
perfection.
We are all God's children.[72]

This is my vision, my hope and my dream.

I truly believe that disabled persons are visual symbols of what
no one wants to be, and of what everyone fears they may
become. Over the years, sharing with Barb about disabilities was a
rare and special privilege. She had that uncanny knack of not only
knowing what to ask, but how and just when to ask it. She knew
the questions, and sometimes even the answers. She was ready to
push any institution to its utmost limits to be a community of
justice. Her legacy to this world will be the incredible population
of women and men who are no longer afraid to analyze and
question, but who do it with great pride, style, and panache. The
greatest part of my vision is that we, in this world, will all learn to
ask questions, to listen to answers and to seek justice wherever
we are. It is no longer good enough for us to accept abuse by the
general public. It is our responsibility to be heard and to help
educate. How else will anyone ever have a chance to learn and to
change?

This questioning and dialoguing and learning and changing must
also happen within the medical profession. Therefore, another
part of my vision concerns them. For those of you who do not
have the good fortune that I have with my doctor, know and own
that it is your body, your life, your disease, and your right and, in
fact, your obligation to ask questions of them. Never be satisfied
with quick, seemingly pat answers, or worse yet, no answers at all.
It is my vision that some day all doctors will treat us as whole
human beings. We are the ones who must be in control of our
lives. We must never be satisfied with anything less than mutual

understanding and the right to decision-making about our body and our life.

It is my vision that someday we will live in a world where we not only know the word justice, but understand its meaning and what we must do for it to be a lifestyle. We must continue to journey towards life, hopes, dreams, and visions being and doing the best with what we have. We need to acknowledge and own our feelings and to take them out and deal with them. In this process we must listen to others, try to understand, and continue to ask questions. We must do all this with openness, honesty and integrity. Only then will we see the rays of sunshine shining through. Some days they are merely glimpses, and some days they are tiny little spots of twinkling light, and some days they encompass the entire world. They are there for us to hold on to, and to help us move forward.

It is my vision that one day we will all be able to say with feeling and meaning: I am a child of God. And with Rosemary Doran we will say:

When I look at you, I am looking for God's image in you.
When you look at me, do you see that image in me?
God grant that I may reflect something of the one who brought me into being.[73]

For me, that is what life is all about: to continue to move towards that equality that God has so powerfully and graciously given to us, and God will once again be able to say, "It is good."

Vision
Joan Heffelfinger

I prepare to see my witch, whose name is Joy, to talk with her about my health. I know we will talk about how I am emotionally, physically, and spiritually. This time, however, I know that she also wants to discuss some test results with me. She has suggested that I might want to bring a friend with me.

So Rob, who is my partner, and I see her together. When we

get to the Wellness Centre, we are warmly received, as we always are. It is a wonderful feeling to be called by name by the host and to be offered something to drink. I also appreciate the fact that we never have to wait to see my witch and she never seems to be in a rush. I always get the sense from talking to Joy that the most important thing in her life at that particular moment is me. What a caring, compassionate person she is! I also thoroughly appreciate the respect with which she treats me. Joy knows that this is my body and that nobody knows as much about it as I do. She never comes across as if she has all the answers.

This time, she needs to share with me some upsetting news, which is that the test results indicate that I have diabetes. In the back of my mind, I had thought as much, but I had been suppressing those thoughts, hoping that it wasn't really so. Joy provides me with much information about diabetes, including simple things that I can do to learn how to live with it. She is also careful, however, not to overload me. Further, she gives me the name of another woman who has the same kind of diabetes as me, a woman who had said that she would love to talk with me. As well, I am given the name of a diabetes educator. Without a doubt, however, the greatest gift my witch gives me is that of listening. She hears me in my shock and anger and deep sorrow over the loss this will mean in my life.

After I share with her all that I am able to for now, she asks Rob if he wants to talk about how he is feeling. He too shares as much as he is able to for the time and then, at his suggestion, she talks with him about ways that he might support me.

When we leave her Healing Space in the Wellness Centre, we go to get the material things that I will need in order to live with diabetes. I remember how as a child, I had to go to one place to see the "doctor" (goodness! It's been a long time since I heard that word!) and another place to pick up my "prescription." (I haven't heard that word for a long time either. It seems so arrogant to me today.) Having all those services in one place makes so much sense.

When I go to pick up the things I need, I remember how as a

child, people had to pay for medicine and all kinds of other paraphernalia related to their "illnesses." It seems so much fairer now that the cost of these things is picked up by the whole of society. Everyone has a certain amount of money each month taken from their pay that is called "coins of compassion." This goes to help make life as full as possible for every person in society.

As I am picking up my things, I notice my friend Alice at the Mobility Centre in the Wellness Centre. She is getting a special basket installed on her wheelchair so that it will be possible for her to transport her baby easily.

I also notice my friend Helen at the Communication Centre. She is getting a new hearing aid. I remember her telling me that this one would easily fit in her ear. I also remember her telling me that she doesn't need it so much anymore since everyone knows sign language. I am so glad that signing is now part of the curriculum in school—excuse me, "centres of creativity." Sometimes the old language is hard to get rid of. Now every child grows up knowing sign language.

When I feel ready, I will be given the opportunity to talk with children about living with diabetes. I know that I am not ready for that yet. I need time to sort out what all of this means for me. Of one thing I am sure. I am not in this alone.

Spiritual Resources

Spiritual resources emerge from the lives of women with disabilities and chronic illnesses. The resources that have become clear to us sometimes grew from traditions of which we are a part and sometimes developed from the realities of our lives. Regardless of denomination, religious affiliation or spiritual practices, central to our spirituality lies the fact that we value our lives. We have come to know the power of Love and of the Holy because of our experiences with our bodies and minds. We have been enriched by sharing together the spiritual paths on which we travel and rest. We know connections with each other, with the Universal and within ourselves that we name holy.

We affirm that women with disabilities are important to the well being of the world. The world needs us and needs to listen to and learn from us. We chart new territory, explore new visions, and create new spiritual resources.

Relationships

For us, spirituality grounds itself in relationships, in community, in connections. As Barb put it, "I have a deep belief that when two people are together, more than one plus one happens." We believe that it is theological to do things together, and that the Spirit works between and among people to keep us connected.

All of us named the value of relationships as significant to our spiritual lives. Friendships, positive family relationships and/or inclusive communities are essential. In them, we tell our stories openly and honestly. Joan's experience seemed significant for many of us:

> The feminist community was the first place that asked me to tell my story of living with a chronic illness. It was also the first community that listened, really listened to me. I firmly believe that much healing comes in telling our stories and breaking the silence. Healing comes in being honest, and in refusing to pretend anymore, particularly in refusing to pretend that everything is okay when it is not.

That same community has taught many women the value of accompaniment. We know that some people find it hard to be in relationships where accompaniment is most needed. Our society focuses on activities, on doing, and on fixing. As I write this chapter, I am going through a series of medical tests. Friends respond in a variety of ways. Some clearly offer accompaniment, the gift of presence as I sort through the implications, fears and possibilities of the potential diagnoses. Others want to do something for me, or to offer hope that it is not really anything serious, or to provide solutions to make my life okay. Some have been silent, not knowing what to say. To be accompanied by silence is better than to be enraged at inappropriate responses.

I am, however, reminded of the tide of feelings associated with disabilities as friends sort through their own feelings around news of potentially disabling conditions, and at their varying signs of relief when the tests have given indication that multiple sclerosis or disintegrating spine are not the source of the problem. At one level I am grateful for people being clear about their own reactions and feelings, and I am grateful to have friends who love me no matter how they react. At another level I wonder, why is it shocking for friends to hear of another's potential for disability?

Elinor's insight that a healthy family (and a healthy society) takes illness in stride is a long way from reality. Our unhealth as a society is shown in our reactions to those who are unhealthy or live with disabilities in our midst. Can not our society accept that chronic illnesses and disabilities happen to many people including our families and friends? A just society with a spirituality of compassion would mean that all who are undergoing tests and newly living with chronic illnesses and disabilities would be accompanied by caring friends and would know that they would continue to have a valuable place in society not determined by physical or mental diagnoses. Presently we count ourselves blessed if we have friends who accompany us and advocates who long and work for a transformed society.

We have said several times that friendships are political. Liz noted, "friendships that can truly accommodate disability fly in the face of the attempt of our society to objectify persons with disabilities." We need communities of friends who love us in our embodied forms and that do accommodate our disabilities. Sometimes all of us, and some of us all the time, need to receive care and assistance from others in order to function freely in society. This means creating new understandings of mutuality in which all of us are free to give and receive in various ways. We need to find new forms of mutuality so that we do not fall into the trap of being helper and helpee, and patterns of charity that leave us objectified. Spiritually and politically we need some level of autonomy and agency in our lives. We do not separate the political and the spiritual. Our integrity, our connectedness, our mutuality, our suffering, and our visions entwine as both political and spiritual.

We name holy those communities without hierarchy that include the diversity of people and experiences that exist in creation. Hierarchical patterns create violence by their nature, whether it be vertical or horizontal violence. We need freedom from hierarchical control, and freedom from the socially constructed pressure to control our bodies to fit a norm we cannot ever fit. All people need to participate in decision-making that affects our lives. When those with disabilities and chronic illnesses set the norms and standards for the whole group, persons who are able and persons with disabilities can participate freely in cooperation and interdependence. We all gain by participating together and by what we all bring. Spiritual communities have the capacity to integrate diverse realities, to connect people to each other, to share love, and to seek justice for those who hold least power in society.

We need to share with some friends along the way who are honest and real and caring. We so much need to nurture and encourage each other. Our spiritual lives are based in loving ourselves and others. In love we know grace. In just relationships, we know that there is great power in Life.

Or as Dorothy and Sharon's song says,

Thank you for love, for holding me, seeing my worth.
Thank you for rage, for sharing my death and urging my birth ....
Strong hearts together, freeing each other,
from prisons dark and old.
New dreams and visions, stirring and boiling,
and cracking those walls of cold.
Thank you for struggle, for grief that is healing my loss and my pain
Thank you for giving me woman's new power to live once again.[74]

Divine Acceptance

Through loving and just relationships we come to know ourselves as a precious part of creation. We believe that all people including those with disabilities are made in God's image. Whatever God is like, we are a part of that. To live in the image of God means self-respect, acceptance, and using our unique gifts creatively and courageously in this world. As Liz so eloquently stated:

For me, hope is believing and expecting that my life has meaning, that I will grow and learn and have fun and love and be loved. It is believing and expecting that my life will be full and interesting, regardless of my physical ability or my health. It is the profound awareness that my body, just as it is, is 'a temple of the Holy Spirit within [me], which [I] have from God' (I Corinthians 6:19) and that as such I am a precious part of creation.

In each chapter women address the common theme of needing to know ourselves as valuable beings just as we are. Mary reminds us that our whole being is holy, "When I am able to accept that all of me is made in God's image, I come closer to realizing that all of me reflects something of God. This is especially true for the parts of me that I try to hide or ignore, my disability, my imperfections. When I accept and love myself as God's beloved creation, formed to be who I am, with potential to grow into my own being, then I am freed to love others, as I come to know that they, too resemble God and are cherished by God." Christine asserts clearly that "My disability is seen by society as a physical flaw but I do not believe that God sees it that way. I think that saying 'God doesn't make junk' is very true. To God, each thing in creation is beautiful because of its uniqueness." And Sharon adds, "What is ours to enjoy is the gift of life from a warm, loving, gracious, and humorous creator, in whose image we are all created."

Those of us who live with disabilities and chronic illnesses value knowing that we are made in the image of the Creator and that we are loved unconditionally by that Creator.

Divine Image

We also re-image God, reframe our perceptions of who/what the One Beyond Us is. We believe that if we are made in the image of God, then the divine reality incorporates our reality.

Again Mary's insight helps:

Each person's picture of what God is like will need to be reworked. If we can see something of God in each neighbour, God cannot be limited to a far away Spirit. If disability mirrors God's image, God must expand to include disability and weakness, as well as perfection and strength. Removing limits from our image of God imposes other limits on our perception of God's abilities.

Mary notes that she does not expect God to move in and fix everything, but this leaves her angry with God's powerlessness. Usually Christian faith focuses on God's omnipotence, that is, God's all-powerfulness. To re-image God as powerless creates difficulty for many people. It means there is no rescuer, no greater power to bring vengeance to our enemies, to those who scorn and mistreat us. To incorporate powerlessness, disability, and weakness into our understanding of the nature of God means that we recognize that God has no more power to change things than do our friends. We can know accompaniment by God, or God as a friend. Gail notes the importance of these images, "However, while I might have felt estranged from my family, I always had a sense that God understood and was holding me in care." While God may long for well-being and justice just as our friends do, we embody God and until our world embodies well-being and justice for all, God's powerlessness is as great as ours. God, like our friends, can simply hold us in understanding and care.

Gail also points out that we are as likely to know the abandonment of God as the accompanying presence of God. In describing her experiences of not graduating even though she had completed her university courses, and of being despised by a congregation member because of her disability, Gail notes that "God had certainly departed" and "I again felt abandoned by God."

As we reframe God's blessing, we also have to reframe sin. Jayne's definition seems helpful: "Sin is the collective attitude of our society that rewards power, violence, betrayal of trust, lies, threats, and violation of persons." It is not sinful is to have a disability, nor to give care and attention to one's body/self, nor to be in painful life circumstances. Sin consists of attitudes and actions that violate and betray, and of social norms and power systems that reward some at the expense of others. Specifically from our point of view, injustice against people with disabilities is sin. We need a reframing of sin in order to respond to Jayne's question: "How can we reframe the power, the shame, the guilt, the fear?" When we stop blaming the victim and instead see sin as misuses of power, we will begin the process of reframing. When we move away from individualism and seeing each individual as responsible for her/his own "misfortune," and create community accountability, we will have begun the process of reframing. When we look at who will gain and who will lose, we will have clearer perspectives on where sin is located.

Justice

We believe that God's aim for all of creation, including humanity, is justice: right relationship and well-being for all, life in all its fullness where people no matter what their class, race, physical or mental ability, sexual orientation, gender, ethnic origin are empowered to be subject of their own lives. Ours is a materialist theology, that is, justice and knowledge of God are rooted in the concrete conditions of human life. Work for justice addresses the real inequities in this world. Social and media images, political thought, and theology all need to move from homogeneity and control over others towards acceptance and diversity where all people affected participate in the naming and the shaping of the common good.

Justice means asking the questions: "What are the alternatives? Who would benefit from this? What will this mean for women? Which women? Where would power be? Would this be oppressive to any group? What are the implications? What are the other options? What would it mean if we could be in solidarity with women around the globe working to transform radically the structures in which we live our lives?"

We think that disability is socially constructed, and that there are others ways of naming varied life experiences and conditions. They do not need to be medicalized or stigmatized. Resources simply need to be placed in different areas of society so that accessibility and freedom to participate are ensured for all. Hierarchies need not separate people who are able from those who have disabilities nor keep a powerful few in control of the resources that are needed by others for basic survival and for full and free life. We want to have broader social constructs and visions of life. As Barb says, "We must be willing to build towards an unknown, step by step, and be willing to risk newness." Or as Sharon puts it, "for me, that is what life is all about: to continue to move towards that equality that God has so powerfully and graciously given to us, and God will once again be able to say, 'it is good.'"

Our Value: Ourselves in This World

Perhaps if we lived in a world where justice reigned, the questions of our value would not have to be addressed. But the world of justice, the social construction of inclusion and diversity, does not yet exist. Thus we need to look at our value, at ourselves in this world.

We dream that we could live ordinary lives. We long for a world where disabilities and chronic illnesses are seen as part of normal life and needed aids to living will be available to all. We fantasize of a world where we would be seen as just happening to live with disabilities and chronic illnesses among our other qualities. We think of a world where we would be invited to tell the truth about our lives: to talk about our chronic illnesses and disabilities as freely as we talk about the movie we have seen or the weather in Saskatchewan.

Our hope would also be that we would have power to make decisions that affect our lives. We have noted that loss of control over one's body and one's days is a part of chronic illness, and this loss provokes deep questions of how to retain agency, how to have any control over one's life and what appropriate control is. Yet we need to be able to recognize that we are still agents in the world even if we cannot control our bodies.

Agency requires a shift from all value being placed on productivity and work. It requires a shift from women's bodies being seen as objects. It requires a shift from making people with disabilities invisible. We must move towards seeing that people with disabilities and chronic illnesses have things to share, have learnings and unique life experiences, have wisdom gained about how to live in the midst of suffering and in the face of death, and that we have a right to participate in the creation of culture. We must know in our whole beings the truth of Liz's words, "Each of us is infinitely precious, not because of what we do or do not do, not because of ability or loss of ability, but because we hold within us the flame of spirit that makes us human. However we name that human spirit breath, as long as we are living, we hold that precious treasure for the whole world."

Through our bodies we know what we know in this world. For us it is a challenge to befriend our bodies, to love ourselves. Yet some days we can hear Elinor's words with grace:

Today she will rest
tend the wounds
allow the pain to flow
from deep within.

Compassion

Mary and Sharon both state strongly that pity from others offers no help. We need the power to be self-defining and self-identified. We need the sense of self-worth that grows out of being respected. Pity takes these away and focuses on what we cannot do because of chronic illnesses or disabilities. Sharon also assert that "things like compassion and respect are very welcomed and cherished" and, as Mary speaks of compassion, she says, "It involves accepting that I am not capable of certain things, and celebrating with me the things that I can do."

We need compassion and solidarity in our collective work for justice-making in the world. We need people who will stand with us, who will advocate for us, and who will encourage communities to accommodate to our needs. We need compassion as we sort our lives and together determine how we can understand each other's embodiment, and enable maximum living, especially as disability increases. We believe that the work of compassion is a needed spiritual discipline in today's world.

Meaning

To be human creates a desire for meaning.

Barb holds up the strength of her life and points out the reality of new forms of meaning that come with increasing disability and encroaching death: "People think that it is all loss, but there have been gains for me in this disability. I see many things differently, see from a different perspective, through a different lens. People, situations, life and death are re-focused from here."

In her chapter, Liz focuses on meaning through the lens of disability. She affirms that hope only comes as we acknowledge pain. Our lives contain pain: for some of us physical and mental pain, for some of us the pain of loss, for some of us the pain of rejection, humiliation, and discrimination, for some of us the pain of despair. But Liz reminds us that knowledge of how to live with pain is one of the spiritual gifts much needed by our world:

> The world needs us: our ideas, our love, our friendship, our very presence. The world is suffering and hurting right now. The world needs now as never before, the voice of those who are learning how to live in hope in the midst of pain. It is important not only for ourselves but to the world that we hold onto the precious treasure that is our life and that we find the way to live with hope in the midst of despair, with peace in the midst of struggle, with courage in the midst of fear.

Living with disabilities and chronic illnesses invites us to face pain, fear, rage, despair, and sometimes death, and to live. We learn how to incorporate loss as spiritual resource and to learn from the searching, hoping, despairing that occur in our lives. In this, spaces for truth-telling about our lives are essential. Out of truth comes the potential for hope.

Our lives signal hope for our world: potential for truth, hope in the midst of despair, peace in the midst of struggle, courage in the midst of fear.

Other Faith Resources

In our work together we have found a number of other faith resources that offer us life and let us know the power of Love and Goodness of Life.

The ability and willingness to question everything undergirds us. Our faith is not based in dogma and belief as much as in the struggle and the exploration. Mary's questions typify this questioning and challenging faith:

> What is the worth of a person? Are some people worth more than others? Does God love non-disabled people more? Are disabled people loved more, because they must be stronger to cope with life? Is it more important to be nice, or nicer to be important? Why do we try to earn love, from God and from humans? Do we also try to earn our love of ourselves? How important is community, and inclusion of those on the fringes and margins?

We believe that the questions keep us going. Sometimes we find answers or insights through resources from religious traditions and through spiritual practices. Sometimes we gain wisdom through our own experiences and reflections, and through the perspectives of others. Sometimes we are simply led to further questions.

Another of the spiritual resources in our lives is anger. We are often angry and our anger empowers us. We try not to suppress the anger we feel in our lives. Rather we use it to fuel our passion for justice, to confront evil when we find it, to wrestle with God and demand a blessing. We believe that we gain health when we can acknowledge and share our anger in communities of accountability and faith.

We also name passion as a spiritual resource. The Ann Mortifee song that Elinor quoted states, "We were born to live, not just survive." All of us care about life. Our impassioned discussion of our lives, of Life, of meaning in this world when we gathered were life-giving for us. It is not always easy to survive and the power and passion that keeps us surviving is not to be minimized. The endurance that enables survival reflects an important spiritual resource for people with chronic illnesses and disabilities. This resource exhibits moral strength and spiritual courage in the boring, exhausting and uncertain times. Our passion for survival and our passionate endurance in the midst of struggle show that we were indeed born to live.

For several of the Barb Wire Collective members, passion frequently gets expressed through music. Listening to, playing, singing music offers life and restoration. Its effects can range from empowerment, to escape from pain, to providing metaphors, to soothing of the savage beast in our souls.

Passion closely connects to creativity. As women with chronic illnesses and disabilities we have to be creative. We invent ways to live in a society that disables us and does not invite our participation. We offer different perspectives on ethical decisions and social issues than those with able bodies and minds. We live with loss and limits; we face fear and life-threatening situations. Out of these come powerful and creative spiritual resources that we share with society.

Our creativity expresses itself in many ways: through music, in writing, in reading, in relationships, in the symbols we discover and use in our lives, sometimes through words, images and dreams. As Elinor points out, "Living with disability takes a lot of ability."

Our social location also teaches us. We are forced to deal with ambiguity and ambivalence. Our bodies do not allow us to live with control or eternal optimism. The messages we get from society conflict. Our religious traditions give us mixed messages. We have the ambiguous advantage of always living on the edges, never quite fitting, but also not caught into the contradictions of privilege of the powerful. The edges do not always provide us with the safety we need, nor are our survival needs always well met. Yet from the edges we can name injustice and stand in solidarity with others who do not have privilege and power in society. From the edges we can question everything and express the doubts and outrage embodied in our faith.

For some of us the Bible, prayer, worship, and other resources from Christian tradition are constructive spiritual resources. Members of the group named the Bible as a helpful resource for getting in touch with anger, for seeing models in the stories of powerful and creative women, in its naming of equality and the value of all people.

The world of nature also provides us with knowledge of our interconnectedness with all of life. As we participate in the world of nature in the diverse ways invited by our disabilities (through observation, or walking, or listening, or connections with animals) we know that we are part of something great.

Humour and play sustain us. Laughter in community restores our souls when we are weary and hopeless. Delight in each other and in creation gives us hope.

As women with varied disabilities and chronic illnesses we have many spiritual resources that assist us in our daily living. Knowing our lives have value, sharing together, being connected to others, to the Universe and having integrity within ourselves are all important. Being spiritual resources to the world which needs our wisdom is also critical. We need to tell our stories honestly, to be accompanied by people who love us, to be in mutual relationships and non-hierarchical communities where we can participate fully and freely.

Our spiritual lives are strong when we believe ourselves to be made in the Divine image, when we see ourselves mirrored in the Holy, and accept ourselves as loved unconditionally by that Creative Spirit. We gain spiritual strength in knowing God as friend, and being able to survive through the times of abandon-ment by God. We have new visions of sin and justice, and new powers of agency as people of value in the world. We offer wisdom to a broken world on how to live with suffering. We draw on the faith resources of our traditions and we invent new ways of entering the presence of the Holy. We expect the gifts of respect, care, advocacy, and solidarity from those around us as we offer models of truth-telling, anger, passion, creativity, and humour that come with living on the edge. It does take a lot of ability to live with disability!

As well, and perhaps most significantly, our experience is central in the spiritual resources of our lives. We offer our lives to you with hope that our stories have touched a chord in your life and thus have become a spiritual resource for you as you share yourself as a spiritual resource in this justice-seeking world.

Endnotes

[1] Mary E. Hunt, "Loving Well Means Doing Justice," in *A Faith of One's Own*, ed. B. Zanotti (Trumansburg, NY: The Crossing Press, 1986), 118.

[2] Mark Rosentraub and John Gilderbloom, "The Invisible Jail," *Social Policy* 20, no. 1 (Summer 1989): 31

[3] Mary Douglas, *Natural Symbols* (London: Barrie and Rockliff, 1970), 65, 70–71.

[4] Susan Wendell, "Towards a Feminist Theory of Disability," *Hypatia* 4, no. 2 (Summer 1989): 113–114.

[5] Mary E. Hunt, *Fierce Tenderness: A Feminist Theology of Friendship* (New York: The Crossroad Publishing Company, 1992), 102.

[6] Susan E. Browne, Debra Connors, and Nanci Stern, "This Body I Love—Finding Ourselves," in *With the Power of Each Breath,* ed. Susan E. Browne, Debra Connors, and Nanci Stern (Pittsburgh: Cleis Press, 1985), 246.

[7] Quoted by Joan Meister, "Keynote Address: The More We Get Together," in *The More We Get Together...,* ed. Houston Stewart, Beth Percival, and Elizabeth Epperly (Charlottetown, PEI: Gynergy Books, 1992), 12–13.

[8] For example, see Christine M. Smith, *Preaching as Weeping, Confession, and Resistance: Radical Responses to Radical Evil* (Louisville: Westminster/John Knox, 1992), 18–19.

[9] Jane Field, "Coming Out of Two Closets," *Canadian Woman Studies* 13, no. 4 (Summer 1993): 18.

[10] Kathy Charmaz, *Good Days, Bad Days: The Self in Chronic Illness and Time* (New Brunswick, NJ: Rutgers University Press, 1991), 15.

[11] Wendell, "Towards a Feminist Theory of Disability," 115.

[12] Adrienne Asch and Michelle Fine, introduction to "Beyond Pedestals," in *Women with Disabilities: Essays in Psychology, Culture and Politics,* ed. Adrienne Asch and Michelle Fine (Philadelphia: Temple University Press, 1988), 29.

[13] Browne, Connors, and Stern "Shut In, Shut Out, Shut Up—Surviving the System," in *With the Power of Each Breath,* 13.

[14] Nancy Eiesland, *The Disabled God: Towards a Liberatory Theology of Disability* (Nashville: Abingdon, 1994), 69.

[15] Smith, 55.

[16] Jean Blomquist, *Wrestling Till Dawn: Awakening to Life in Times of Struggle* (Nashville: Upper Room Books, 1994), 59–60.

[17] Eiesland, 75.

[18] Eiesland, 101.

[19] Smith, 36.

[20] Kwok Pui-lan, "Mothers and Daughters, Writers and Fighters," in *Inheriting Our Mothers' Gardens,* ed. Letty M. Russell, Kwok Pui-lan, Ada Maria Isai-Diaz, and Katie Geneva Canon (Philadelphia: Westminster, 1988), 32.

[21] Eiesland, 67.

[22] See Sharon Welch, *Communities of Resistance and Solidarity* (Maryknoll: Orbis, 1985) for a fuller discussion of this idea.

[23] Amanecida Collective, *Revolutionary Forgiveness* (Maryknoll: Orbis, 1987), xxxiii.

[24] I am thankful to Nathaniel Branden, who writes about the concept of living consciously in *How to Raise Your Self-Esteem* (New York: Bantam Books Inc., 1988).

[25] Mary E. Hunt, *Fierce Tenderness.*

[26] From "Sister, Friend," *Class Act* (Toronto: On the Line Music Collective, 692 Coxwell Avenue, M4C 3B6, OTL-004, 1986), audiocassette.

[27] Judy Kaye, "A River of Birds," *A Circle is Cast* (Cambridge, MA.: Libana, P.O. Box 530, 02140, Spinning Records SRC-002, 1986), audiocassette.

[28] Marjory H. Shaevitz, *Superwoman Syndrome* (New York: Warner Books, 1984).

[29] Dorthee Soelle, *Suffering* (Philadelphia: Fortress Press, 1975), 92.

[30] Joan Turner has written about her work in *Healing Voices: Feminist Approaches to Therapy with Women,* ed. Toni Ann Laidlaw, Cheryl Malmo, and Associates (San Francisco: Jossey Bass Publishers, 1990).

[31] Jean Illsley Clarke and Carole Gesme, *Oval Affirmations: 139 Ways to Give and Get Affirmations* (Plymouth, MN: Daisy Press, 16535-9th Avenue West, 55447). Affirmations ovals are available as laminated coloured ovals in pocket, table, or wall sizes, or as bookmarks. Each set contains 54 developmental affirmations. They can be ordered from Carole Gesme, 4036 Kerry Court, Minnekota, MN. 55345.

[32] Jean Illsley Clarke and Connie Dawson, *Growing Up Again: Parenting Ourselves, Parenting our Children,* Hazelden, 1989, 122.

[33] Ann Mortifee, "Born to Live," *Born to Live* (West Vancouver, BC: Mahela Music, Jabula Records, P.O. Box 91699, V7V 3P3).

[34] For more information about and examples of visualizations, see Diane Mariechild, *Motherwit* (Trumansburg: The Crossing Press, 1981) and Crystal Visions (Trumansburg: The Crossing Press, 1985) or John Callanan, *God in All Things: The Spiritual Exercises of Anthony De Mello* (New York: Bantam Doubleday Dell Publishing Group, 1994) and Anthony De Mello, *The Song of the Bird* (New York: Doubleday, 1982).

[35] Alla Renee Bozarth, *Life is Goodbye Life is Hello; Grieving Well Through All Kinds of Loss* (Minneapolis MN: Comp Care Publishers, 1986), 166.

[36] Rosemary Doran, "In the Image of God," in *Images of Ourselves: The Faith and Work of Canadian Women,* compiled by The Canadian Ecumenical Decade Coordinating Group for The Ecumenical Decade of Churches in Solidarity with Women in Church and Society (Toronto: The United Church Publishing House, 1992), 81–83.

[37] WOMANSURGE, words Dorothy Logan; music Sharon Davis copyright 1981, unpublished.

[38] As cited in Lois Klempa, "Good News for Modern Women," in *Images of Ourselves,* 31–33.

[39] JoAnne Walter, "Images of Myself," in *Images of Ourselves,* 68.

[40] Committee on Worship, *Service Book* (Toronto: The United Church of Canada and Canec Publishing and Supply House, 1986).

[41] Joyce Carlson, editor, *The Dancing Sun: A Cross Cultural Resource for Strengthening Families,* Vol. IV (Toronto: First Nations Ecumenical Liturgical Resources, Anglican Church of Canada, and The United Church of Canada, 1994).

[42] Christine Smith and Burton Cooper elaborate on the idea of a disabled God. See Christine M. Smith, *Preaching as Weeping, Confession, and Resistance,* chapter 1; and Burton Cooper, "The Disabled God," *Theology Today* 49, no. 2 (July 1992).

[43] Blomquist, 62.

[44] Charmaz, 149

[45] Charmaz, 119.

[46] Susan Wendell, "Feminism, Disability and Transcendence of the Body," *Canadian Woman Studies* 13, no. 4 (Summer 1993): 120.

[47] Eleanor H. Haney, *Vision & Struggle: Meditations on Feminist Spirituality and Politics* (Portland, ME: Astarte Shell Press, 1989), 15.

[48] Maggie Burston, "Sick But Not Silenced," *Candida Research and Information Foundation* Issue 1 (1989): 7.

[49] Joanne Carlson Brown and Rebecca Parker, "For God So Loved the World?" in *Christianity, Patriarchy and Abuse,* ed. Joanne Carlson Breown and Carol R. Bohn (New York: The Pilgrim Press, 1989).

[50] Smith, 18–19.

[51] Sharon D. Stone, "Must Disability Always Be Visible," *Canadian Woman Studies* 13, no. 4 (Summer 1993): 12.

[52] Mary Daly uses this concept in several places. See Mary Daly, *Gyn/Ecology* (Boston: Beacon, 1978), especially 1–34; and *Pure Lust* (Boston: Beacon, 1984), 146–150.

[53] *Unbeaten Paths* is available through the Saskatchewan Christian Feminist Network, 418 A McDonald St., Regina, SK S4N 6E1.

[54] Cheri Register, *Living with Chronic Illness: Days of Patience and Passion* (New York: Bantam, 1987), 192.

[55] The Mudflower Collective, *God's Fierce Whimsy* (New York: Pilgrim Press, 1985), 108–113, especially 112.

[56] Nelle Morton, *The Journey Is Home* (Boston: Beacon, 1985), 157–158.

[57] Bonnie Klein on CBC radio "Centerpoint" (October 11, 1992).

[58] Morton, 55.

[59] Carter Heyward, *When Boundaries Betray Us: Beyond Illusions of What is Ethical in Therapy and Life* (New York: HarperCollins, 1993).

[60] Oliver Sacks, *A Leg to Stand On* (London: Pan Books, Picador), 1986.

[61] Carolyn McDade, "Woman to Woman," *Sister Carry On* (Wellfleet, MA: Carolyn McDade, 1992), audiocassette.

[62] Carole R. Fontaine, "Roundtable Discussion: Women with Disabilities," *Journal of Feminist Studies in Religion* 10, no. 2 (Fall 1994): 109.

[63] Connors, "Disability, Sexism and the Social Order," in *With the Power of Each Breath*, 92–93.

[64] Elizabeth O'Connor, "Learnings from An Illness," *Journal of Christian Healing* 10 (Fall 1988): 3.

[65] Starhawk, *Truth or Dare: Encounters with Power, Authority and Mystery* (San Francisco: Harper and Row, 1990), 145.

[66] Charmaz, 138.

[67] Elisabeth Kubler-Ross, *On Death and Dying* (New York: The MacMillan Company, 1969).

[68] Franklin Shontz, "Body Image and Physical Disability," in *Body Images: Development, Deviance and Change,* ed. Thomas F. Cash and Thomas Pruzinsky (New York: The Guilford Press, 1990), 167.

[69] Bernice Fisher and Roberta Galler, "Friendship and Fairness: How Disability Affects Friendship between Women," in *Women with Disabilities*, 180.

[70] Margo Adair, *Working Inside Out: Tools for Change* (Berkeley CA: Wingbow Press, 1984), 336.

[71] This theme emerges in passages such as Psalm 41, Isaiah 55:6–13, Isaiah 60, Luke 12:22–31, II Corinthians 6:2, and Revelation 21:1–7.

[72] Doran, 81.

[73] Doran, 83.

[74] WOMANSURGE.

About the Authors

Charlotte Caron is a feminist activist and spiritual leader in Saskatchewan. She is currently Co-president and Professor of Pastoral Theology at St. Andrew's Theological College in Saskatoon, Saskatchewan. Her writing includes several articles about chronic illness in feminist journals. She spent the sabbatical year, 1996–97 as Visiting Scholar at the Centre for Feminist Research at York University writing about women and loss as well as about worship in The United Church of Canada.

Gail Christy was ordained to ministry in 1983. She has served in Saskatchewan and is currently serving Riceville-Pendleton Pastoral Charge in Eastern Ontario and the Elizabeth Bruyere Health Centre in Ottawa as the United Church Chaplain. She also occasionally returns to her old life as a counsellor at a community college in Ottawa.

Sharon Davis has travelled extensively in Europe and Canada. She lived briefly in Newfoundland and Ontario, but she has feelings of great pride about spending 23 of her 25 years in paid accountable ministry in Saskatchewan where she was born and raised. Currently she is on staff at St. James United Church in Regina, where she continues to work at asking "those questions."

Mary Elford is an ordained minister of The United Church of Canada, currently serving in Saskatchewan. Though she is no stranger to reading and writing, this is her first published piece.

Joan Heffelfinger is a friend, a feminist, a person of faith, a mom, a partner, and a paid accountable minister. On her tombstone she would like to see the words "compassion" and "zest for life." Joan feels blessed to be part of the Barb Wire Collective where she has learned again that friendship is about being with each other in pain, and laughing and raging together. In the midst of that, there can be a blessing.

Elinor Johns is a teacher and an explorer of many dimensions of health and healing. She is creating a home-based business as a representative of Sunrider International, a herbal whole food company. She lives in Winnipeg with her three children.

Christine Neal graduated from University of Saskatchewan and completed her clinical dietician internship in Hamilton, Ontario. She spent a challenging and rewarding year working at an orphanage in Bolivia. She currently practises as a dietician in Saskatchewan.

Liz Richards enjoys living with her family in the beauty of rural Saskatchewan where she serves two congregations of The United Church of Canada as an ordained minister. She has previously lived and worked as a nurse in Alberta and Yukon as well as Saskatchewan. She is currently writing a thesis on counselling and disabilities for her Master of Pastoral Counselling degree.

Jayne Whyte identifies herself first as a friend, then as writer, speaker, and mental health consumer advocate living in Fort Qu'Appelle, Saskatchewan. She leads worship one Sunday each month in the United Church of Canada at Edgeley. She recently began a career as researcher and resource in areas of mental health, disability, poverty and social change.